CAMBRIDGE MUSIC HANDBOOKS

Gershwin: *Rhapsody in Blue*

CAMBRIDGE MUSIC HANDBOOKS

GENERAL EDITOR Julian Rushton

Cambridge Music Handbooks provide accessible introductions to major musical works.

Published titles

Bach: *The Brandenburg Concertos* MALCOLM BOYD
Bach: Mass in B Minor JOHN BUTT
Bartók: *Concerto for Orchestra* DAVID COOPER
Beethoven: *Missa solemnis* WILLIAM DRABKIN
Beethoven: *Pastoral Symphony* DAVID WYN JONES
Beethoven: Symphony No. 9 NICHOLAS COOK
Berg: Violin Concerto ANTHONY POPLE
Berlioz: *Roméo et Juliette* JULIAN RUSHTON
Brahms: *A German Requiem* MICHAEL MUSGRAVE
Brahms: Symphony No. 1 DAVID BRODBECK
Britten: *War Requiem* MERVYN COOKE
Chopin: The Four Ballades JIM SAMSON
Debussy: *La mer* SIMON TREZISE
Gershwin: *Rhapsody in Blue* DAVID SCHIFF
Handel: *Messiah* DONALD BURROWS
Haydn: *The Creation* NICHOLAS TEMPERLEY
Haydn: String Quartets, Op. 50 W. DEAN SUTCLIFFE
Holst: *The Planets* RICHARD GREENE
Ives: *Concord Sonata* GEOFFREY BLOCK
Janáček: *Glagolitic Mass* PAUL WINGFIELD
Liszt: Sonata in B Minor KENNETH HAMILTON
Mahler: Symphony No. 3 PETER FRANKLIN
Mendelssohn: *The Hebrides* and other overtures R. LARRY TODD
Mozart: Clarinet Concerto COLIN LAWSON
Mozart: The 'Jupiter' Symphony ELAINE R. SISMAN
Musorgsky: *Pictures at an Exhibition* MICHAEL RUSS
Nielsen: Symphony No. 5 DAVID FANNING
Schoenberg: *Pierrot lunaire* JONATHAN DUNSBY
Schubert: *Die schöne Müllerin* SUSAN YOUENS
Schumann: Fantasie, Op. 17 NICHOLAS MARSTON
Sibelius: Symphony No. 5 JAMES HEPOKOSKI
Strauss: *Also sprach Zarathustra* JOHN WILLIAMSON
Stravinsky: *Oedipus rex* STEPHEN WALSH
Verdi: Requiem DAVID ROSEN
Vivaldi: *The Four Seasons* and other concertos, Op. 8 PAUL EVERETT

Gershwin: *Rhapsody in Blue*

David Schiff
Reed College, Portland, Oregon

PUBLISHED BY THE PRESS SYNDICATE OF THE UNIVERSITY OF CAMBRIDGE
The Pitt Building, Trumpington Street, Cambridge CB2 1RP, United Kingdom

CAMBRIDGE UNIVERSITY PRESS
The Edinburgh Building, Cambridge CB2 2RU, United Kingdom
40 West 20th Street, New York, NY 10011–4211, USA
10 Stamford Road, Oakleigh, Melbourne 3166, Australia

First published 1997

Printed in the United Kingdom at the University Press, Cambridge

Typeset in Ehrhardt MT 10½/13

A catalogue record for this book is available from the British Library

Library of Congress cataloguing in publication data

Schiff, David.
Gershwin, Rhapsody in blue/David Schiff.
p. cm. – (Cambridge music handbooks)
Includes bibliographical references and index.
ISBN 0 521 55077 7 (hardback) – ISBN 0 521 55953 7 (paperback)
1. Gershwin, George, 1898–1937. Rhapsody in blue. I. Title.
II. Series.
ML 410.G288S27 1997
784.2'62–dc21 96–47439 CIP MN

ISBN 0 521 55077 7 (hardback)
ISBN 0 521 55953 7 (paperback)

SN

Contents

Acknowledgments

My first thanks should go to the record companies who have made it so easy to hear the entire history of *Rhapsody in Blue* at home, but I have many important personal thanks as well. I was greatly helped by Wayne Shirley, Music Librarian of the Library of Congress, who allowed me to see the manuscript score of the *Rhapsody*, and shared his wisdom on many related subjects, especially novelty piano. Carol Oja and Mark Tucker graciously took time away from their many scholarly projects to give my manuscript a close reading. Their comments and questions were a great assistance in the final revisions of the book. Michael Tilson Thomas very kindly shared his insights into Gershwin's music, his milieu and his personality. Phyllis Birnbaum searched Widener Library at Harvard for information on Isaac Goldberg. My editor Julian Rushton has been a constant prod to clarity and I hope that I have managed to heed his warning against sounding parochial. Penny Souster has been a great source of encouragement and a dear friend. Reed College helped me with travel expenditures and granted me a sabbatical so that I could write the book. Betty Woerner, media librarian at Reed, tracked down articles and rare recordings. Jay Cohen helped me prepare the bibliography. My family, Judy, Daniel and Jamie have nobly put up with a year of Gershwin blasting through the house and a grumpy writer chasing them off the premises. I could not have done it without them.

I

Introduction: the one and only

> I don't think this music could be devalued. It has such character of its own, I don't think anything could kill it.
>
> Leopold Godowsky III, son of Frances Gershwin Godowsky.

In 1987, United Airlines agreed to pay an annual fee of $300,000 for the rights to use Gershwin's *Rhapsody in Blue* in its advertisements, the first time the work was ever licensed for such a purpose. According to *The Washington Post*:[1] "One of the first commercials using the rhapsody features its familiar, romantic, dah-dah-dahhhh-dah theme over shots of business persons bustling around offices and airports." Six months afterwards, the *Rhapsody*, already one of the most frequently performed concert works of the twentieth century, was played – behind the husky voice of Gene Hackman – in United commercials throughout the 1988 Summer Olympics. It muffled the engine noise on United flights preparing for takeoff and upon landing, and floated through the busy passenger tunnel connecting United's two concourses at O'Hare Airport in Chicago – America's busiest. Apparently United chose the *Rhapsody* more for its cultural resonances than for its actual notes. Pursuant to the licensing agreement, the airline used the tunes of *Rhapsody in Blue* reordered and reorchestrated for its own purposes. *The Washington Post* observed that "had the family refused permission, the advertiser could have commissioned an original composition made to sound so much like the *Rhapsody* that many people would have thought that's what they were hearing."[2] A few years later Delta Airlines, one of United's rivals, began to use the big Gershwinesque tune from Rakhmaninov's *Rhapsody on a Theme of Paganini* as its theme song. Since the E-major theme of *Rhapsody in Blue* has always reminded listeners of Tchaikovsky, its stand-in by Rakhmaninov would seem to affirm Gershwin's Russian origins, but as marketing tools both Gershwin's theme and Rakhmaninov's functioned as emblems of soaring Americanism.

Despite its enduring popularity, or because of it, the *Rhapsody* remains controversial – and this handbook will examine many of the controversies. We might divide the areas of dispute into issues of form and context – though they overlap. Unlike most classical compositions, the *Rhapsody* exists in several different published versions, and has been recorded in even more diverse variants. This creates a certain unresolvable confusion as to the identity of the *Rhapsody* and it has also opened the work up to accusations of formlessness, though its problem may be an overabundance of forms. Many critics have described it as a loosely ordered sequence of tunes. The identity of the piece, as Leonard Bernstein and others have argued, lies in the melodies, not their sequence.[3] As mere description this has some validity, given the proliferation of versions which contain from one to five of the original themes in differing orders. But as an aesthetic judgment – which it usually becomes – the accusation of formlessness rests on a priori notions of formal integrity and thematic development which cast the *Rhapsody* in the dubious position of not being a composition at all. The fact that the *Rhapsody* has outlived many works whose compositional credentials have never been questioned raises an interesting aesthetic issue: if a musical work continues to be played for three generations after its première just how flawed can its form be?

Viewed as a type of composition rather than on its own terms the *Rhapsody* resists classification. At its appearance critics saw it as an example either of jazz or of modern music – or both. It was, after all, premièred by a famous jazz band at a concert entitled "An Experiment in Modern Music." As we shall see, this judgment was a function of the delayed appearances in New York of both European modernist music and New Orleans jazz. Soon after the *Rhapsody*'s February 1924 première, with the arrival of Aaron Copland from Paris and Louis Armstrong from Chicago, the *Rhapsody* began to seem extraneous to the evolutions of both modern music and jazz. The European jazz craze which produced *Parade*, *L'histoire du soldat*, and *La création du monde* quickly faded, as did the vogue for symphonic jazz which was led by Paul Whiteman. Gradually, the *Rhapsody* moved into the symphonic repertory, helped along by Ferde Grofé's revised scoring for (more or less) standard orchestra.

In a century characterized by the unpopularity of its most prestigious music, the popular success of the *Rhapsody* has made it suspect. Critics might accept it as a better example of light music, but would not place it next to the works of Stravinsky, Schoenberg or Bartók. Or, worse, they deemed it bad art masquerading as the real thing – kitsch. The persistence of the classification problem points to the hardening of musical categories in this century, as popular and high forms differentiated themselves from each other. Despite this tendency, "high" composers have pursued projects of *gebrauchsmusik* and other ways of returning to the everyday world or abolishing the supposed boundaries between art and life, and pop musicians from Gershwin to Benny Goodman, Frank Zappa and Paul McCartney have tried to cross over into the classical area. Gershwin's success in both fields, however, remains unique. Although Gershwin was never considered a jazz performer he has contributed to jazz in two ways: as a composer of jazz standards like "I Got Rhythm," "Embraceable You" and "Summertime," and as a composer of concert works whose idiom derives from jazz. Undoubtedly Gershwin's huge success in both areas overshadowed the parallel accomplishments of such African-American artists as James P. Johnson, Fats Waller, William Grant Still and even Duke Ellington. Jazz writers, both black and white, have accused him of gross appropriation of an idiom that was not rightfully his. They cite the *Rhapsody* as a prime example of commercially successful fake jazz, part of a long history of cultural theft from Stephen Foster's plantation songs to the Beastie Boys' white rap. While the facts of racial injustice are indisputable, however, the relation of black and white musicians in the formation of the many musical styles associated with jazz is a complex subject. In music, appropriation is often the sincerest form of admiration. *Rhapsody in Blue* is an enduring monument to the love affair of Americans – and people around the world – with the African-American idiom that became the most influential language of twentieth-century music.

2

Identity

> Rhapsody in Blue is not a real composition in the sense that whatever happens in it must seem inevitable, or even pretty inevitable. You can cut out parts of it without affecting the whole in any way except to make it shorter. You can remove any of these stuck-together sections and the piece still goes on as bravely as before. You can even interchange these sections with one another and no harm is done. You can make cuts within a section, or add new cadenzas, or play it with any combination of instruments or on the piano alone; it can be a five-minute piece or a six-minute piece, or a twelve-minute piece. And in fact all these things are being done to it every day. It's still the Rhapsody in Blue.[1]

Before talking about *Rhapsody in Blue* we need to specify our object of study – which is no easy task. There are five published versions of the (more or less) complete work:

(1) "george gershwin's rhapsody in blue two pianos-four hands (original)." Warner Brothers PSO165. "Dedicated to Paul Whiteman." This corresponds roughly to the score that Gershwin gave Ferde Grofé to orchestrate. Despite the "original" in the title it appears to have been edited, with the addition of rehearsal letters, for example, to be used as a soloist's part with the miniature orchestral score (3) rather than the original jazz-band version. At rehearsal 4, moreover, the two-piano score follows the later orchestration (3) rather than the original by omitting the accompaniment. There is an introduction by Henry Levine explaining "characteristic rhythmic figures."

(2) "George Gershwin Rhapsody in Blue Commemorative Facsimile Edition," 1987. Gershwin 50th Anniversary Edition Warner Brothers FS0004. There is a photo offset of Ferde Grofé's original score for the Whiteman Band, and there are notes by Jeff Sultanof. This version contains some passages cut before publication. The solo piano part is not

complete; there was no need, or time, for Grofé to copy it out in full. The Whiteman band, according to a list in the score, consisted of twenty-three musicians:

Reeds:
Ross Gorman: E-flat & B-flat soprano saxophones, alto saxophone, oboe, heckelphone, E-flat soprano clarinet, B-flat clarinet, alto and bass clarinet octavion [*sic*]
Hale Byers: B-flat soprano saxophone, tenor saxophone, baritone saxophone, flute
Donald Clark: B-flat soprano saxophone, alto saxophone, baritone saxophone

Brass:
Trumpets and flugelhorns: Henry Busse, Frank Siegrist
French horns: A. Cerino, A. Corrado
Trombones: Roy Maxon (= euphonium) and James Casseday (+Bass trombone)
Tuba and string bass: Gus Helleburg, Albert Armer

Piano: Ferde Grofé, Henry Lange (+Celeste)

Banjo: Michael Pingatore

Drums, timpani and traps: George Marsh

Violins: Alex Drasein (Concert master), George Torde, Robert Berchad, Kurt Dieterle, Joseph Streisof, Jack Eaton, Bert Hirsh, Mario Perry (+accordion)

(3) "george gershwin's RHAPSODY IN BLUE miniature orchestra score. Warner Brothers M00013. Scored by Ferde Grofé." Dated 1942. Scored for 2 flutes, 2 oboes, 2 B-flat clarinets, bass clarinet in B flat, 2 bassoons, 3 horns in F, 3 trumpets in B flat, three trombones, tuba, timpani, "drums" (percussion), 2 alto saxophones in E flat, tenor saxophone in B flat, banjo, strings. A foreword by Frank Campbell-Watson suggests (puzzlingly) that the saxophone and banjo parts are "almost optional." According to the notes in (2) this arrangement is based on one Grofé made in 1926 for the standard theater orchestra of the day (unpublished), with single flute, oboe and bassoon, 2 horns,

2 trumpets and trombone. Although many of the solos remain the same, many others are now doubled.

(4) "george gershwin's RHAPSODY IN BLUE piano solo." Dated 1924. Warner Brothers PS0047. Foreword by F. C. W. This is a piano-solo score which, however, differs from the version Gershwin recorded on piano rolls. It cuts the music from rehearsal 14 to four bars before 19 and from two bars before rehearsal 22 to five after 24. It also authorizes optional cuts from four bars before rehearsal 19 to four before 25 and from two before 32 to six before 33.

(5) "george gershwin's rhapsody in blue piano duet arranged after the original score by henry levine." Warner Brothers PS0157. The foreword by F. C. W. says "the present setting for Piano Duet of the Rhapsody in Blue was made by Henry Levine, one of the few privileged to study the work with Gershwin himself. Mr. Levine has based his transcription entirely on the original score, admitting of no departures of fanciful interpolations tending to distort the concept of the composer." Copyright 1943.

In addition there are several published versions of the "main theme" from *Rhapsody in Blue* as a simplified piano solo (as well as for many other instruments). The 1939 Gotham Classics edition of *Rhapsody in Blue* "adapted for Studio and Home" by Henry Levine advertises arrangements of the work for violin, organ, accordion and symphony band, with a version of the "Andante and Finale" for violin and piano, violin, cello and piano, clarinet and piano, alto saxophone and piano and, of all things, organ (Hammond and Pipe) and piano.

Versions (1), (3) and (5) correspond in bar count. Versions (1) and (3) share rehearsal letters. Because it contains the complete piano part and rehearsal numbers, the miniature orchestra score (3) will serve as a frame of reference in this book.

Versions (1), (4) and 5 sanction various cuts (see Table 1). Although these cuts seem to be based on considerations either of thematic repetition or the avoidance of a few technically difficult passages, their origin, motivation and status are not clear. The publisher may have wanted to create a one-size-fits-all work which could be played in versions lasting from five to sixteen minutes. None of the cuts sanctioned in versions (1) and (4) appears in Gershwin's recorded performances. Gershwin's recordings, however, do contain substantial cuts, as do those by Oscar

Levant and Leonard Bernstein. Only in recent years has it become standard practice to perform the work "as written," often in versions that claim to be the original Whiteman band arrangement.

Table 1.

Column A: Bar numbers in 1, 2, 3, 5
Column B: Rehearsal numbers in 1, 3
Column C: Optional cuts in 1: A TO B; C TO D; E TO F; G TO H
Column D: Bars omitted from 4: X TO Y
Column E: Optional cuts in 4: O TO P
Column F: Optional cuts in 5: A TO B; C TO D
Column G: Cuts in 1924 recording
Column H: Cuts in Levant recording
Column I: Cuts in Bernstein 1958 recording
Column J: Themes and cadenzas

Introduction

A	B	C	D	E	F	G	H	I	J
1									
2									Ritornello
11	[1]								
16	[2]								
18									
									Tag
20									
21	[3]								Ritornello
24	[4]								Tag
30		(A)							Cadenza I
38									Ritornello (solo)
40									
41	[5]								(Tag)
46									(Tag)
55									Cadenza II
65		(B)							
72	[6]								Ritornello (tutti)
74									
75									(Tag)
81	[7]								
85	[8]								

Scherzo

A	B	C	D	E	F	G	H	I	J
91	[9]								Train
99	[10]								
105	[11]								
108									Link
115	[12]								Stride
130	[13]								Link
138	[14]		X			X		X	Shuffle
146	[15]								
158	[16]								
166	[17]								
172	[18]					Y		Y	Link (piano)
177			Y	O					
181	[19]	(C)							Stride (solo)
196	[20]					X			
215	[21]								
223					A		X		Ritornello
225									
226			X					X	
228	[22]								Ritornello ("trio")
236	[23]								
243	[24]						Y	Y	Cadenza 3
248			Y						
256		(D)		P	B				
260	[25]								Shuffle (solo)
276	[26]	(E)							
297	[27]								Grand cadenza
298						Y			
299		(F)							

Slow movement

A	B	C	D	E	F	G	H	I	J
303	[28]								Love
321	[29]								
325	[30]								
343	[31]								
345				O					
347	[32]								Link (piano)
357									Love (solo)
377				P					

Finale

A	B	C	D	E	F	G	H	I	J
383	[33]				(C)				
387		(G)				X			
411									Tag
414						Y			
423		(H)			(D)				
425	[34]								Love
433	[35]								
449	[36]								
461	[37]								Tag
471	[38]								
487	[39]		X				X		Stride
488			Y						
500							Y		
504	[40]								Ritornello
508									Tag
510									

The identity of *Rhapsody in Blue* as a "property" further complicates the story, since as Bernstein suggests it is often heard in fragmentary versions with many different kinds of arrangements. The Whiteman band used the E-major "Love" tune as its theme song, and other fragments of the piece were used as background music even before United Airlines turned it into a jingle. According to copyright law any one of these manifestations is still the *Rhapsody*.[2] This legal definition frames the work as a compendium of five tunes plus a recurring motivic tag, and any one of these six melodic elements stands for the whole. Significantly, Carla Michelotti, the lawyer who negotiated on behalf of United Airlines with Warner Music for the rights, referred to the work as a "song": "This is a song that is a very special song for everyone, and we wanted to treat it special."[3]

Both published orchestrations are problematic. Grofé's "original" version was premised on the personalities and doubling abilities of the Whiteman band. The full orchestra version introduces doublings that obscure the idiomatic colors of the original. At rehearsal 14, for example, the original gives the melody to the clarinet, baritone sax, banjo, tuba and band piano – a jazz sonority; the full version assigns the melody to bass clarinet, bassoons, three saxophones, cellos and basses – a mixed jazz/classical sonority. Many of these doublings render the saxophone and banjo parts redundant. Since most orchestras contain neither color, the "full" score allows for performances without them. The full score, therefore, might be treated as an overscoring, allowing for different interpretations.

Aside from inconsistencies between the published scores, the identity of *Rhapsody in Blue* remains unstable. As the scoring evolved from "jazz band" to "pit orchestra" to symphony orchestra – albeit with saxophones and banjo – the stylistic center of gravity of the work also changed. In the original scoring the band is playing jazz while the piano introduces classical elements; in the symphonic version the orchestra seems to be the classical element while the soloist takes on the burden of sounding "jazzy." Most often the work appears in a "pops" concert framework, which has its own style of performance. The *Rhapsody* lives on both as a fully composed piano concerto, usually played, as is the fashion today, in some purportedly "authentic" manner, and as a medley of detachable melodies – several of which are not so easily detached.

The rapid creation of the *Rhapsody* has left some doubt as to the identity of its creator(s). In later years there was some acrimony between Grofé and Gershwin, or their estates. Gershwin wrote a letter to ASCAP – which now hangs on the wall of its board room – reminding the organization that the *Rhapsody* was his piece "no matter what Ferde Grofé tells you." In a letter published in *Singing* (October 1926) Gershwin wrote that "Grofé worked from a very complete piano and orchestral sketch in which many of the orchestral colors were indicated."[4] In later years Grofé stated that Gershwin lacked the ability to orchestrate at the time despite his lessons with Goldmark.[5]

Gershwin told Isaac Goldberg that he had his first ideas about the *Rhapsody* even before he went to Boston for the première, or possibly one of the try-outs, of *Sweet Little Devil*; the trip to Boston may have been as early as 20 December 1923 or just after the New Year.[6] According to a story which may have been invented later to explain why Gershwin did not score the *Rhapsody*, he forgot about Whiteman's year-old commission until he read about it in the newspapers on 4 January 1924.[7] According to Jablonski[8] Gershwin completed work on the two-piano score of the *Rhapsody* no later than 29 January 1924, when he played in a recital given in Boston by Eva Gauthier (there is no completion date on the manuscript). His score contained some indications of instruments, but not enough to allow a merely mechanical transcription; some of these indications may be in Grofé's hand. Charles Schwartz claims that the final score ignores many of these indications, but he overstates the case. Grofé consulted with Gershwin while he was completing the piece and began scoring it from sketches while it was in progress, page by page.[9] Grofé completed the scoring on 4 February. Gershwin never claimed to have orchestrated the piece; Grofé never claimed to have done anything more than orchestrate it. (In most of his arrangements for the Whiteman band, Grofé's work went well beyond mere instrumentation.) Grofé's intimate knowledge of the band's personnel contributed to the success of the piece, but the *Rhapsody* has outlived the Whiteman band.

The identities of the two later arrangements still raise questions, however. Gershwin claimed that he orchestrated the *Concerto in F* in 1925.[10] The *Concerto* is quite competently scored (although, as Wayne Shirley indicates, not flawlessly) for full orchestra, indicating either that Gershwin actually could have orchestrated the *Rhapsody* the year before, or that he had mastered orchestration in the course of the year – or, as rumors had it, that he was substantially assisted in scoring the Concerto by friends like Bill Daly – rumors denied by Daly in 1933.[11] Assuming that Gershwin in fact was primarily responsible for orchestrating the *Concerto* in 1925, why then did he not make his own orchestral version of the *Rhapsody* after that time? Since such an arrangement would have been worth a lot of money we can only guess that Grofé retained legal rights to any scoring of the piece. The *Rhapsody* remains a collaboration.

3

Instruction manual (instead of an analysis)

Suddenly an idea occurred to me. There had been so much talk about the limitations of jazz, not to speak of the manifest misunderstanding of its function. Jazz, they said, had to be in strict time. It had to cling to dance rhythms. I resolved, if possible, to kill the misconception with one sturdy blow. Inspired by this aim, I set to work composing. I had no set plan, no structure to which my music must conform. The *Rhapsody*, you see, began as a purpose, not a plan. I worked out a few themes, but just at this time I had to appear in Boston for the premiere of Sweet Little Devil. It was on the train, with its steely rhythms, its rattlety-bang that is often so stimulating to a composer (I frequently hear music in the very heart of noise), that I suddenly heard – even saw on paper – the complete construction of the Rhapsody, from beginning to end. . . . No new themes came to me, but I worked on the thematic material already in my mind, and tried to conceive the composition as a whole. I heard it as sort of a musical kaleidoscope of America – of our vast melting pot, of our incomparable national pep, our blues, our metropolitan madness. By the time I reached Boston I had a definite plot of the piece, as distinguished from its actual substance. The middle theme came to me suddenly, as music oftentimes does. It was at the home of a friend, just after I got back to Gotham. I must do a great deal of subconscious composing, and this is an example. Playing at parties is one of my notorious weaknesses. Well, as I was playing, without a thought of the *Rhapsody*, all at once I heard myself playing a theme that must have been haunting me inside, seeking outlet. No sooner had it oozed out of my fingers that I realized I had found it. Within a week of my return from Boston I had completed the structure, in the rough, of the *Rhapsody in Blue*.[1]

Finding in his notebook a theme (the clarinet glissando) which he thought might make an appropriate opening for a more extended work than he had been accustomed to writing, he decided to chance it.[2]

> Carried along by Whiteman's enthusiasm and encouragement, Gershwin, in his free moments from the show, pored through his "Tune Books" for some suitable ideas and on Monday January 7, began writing . . . he abandoned his original title, American Rhapsody, at Ira's suggestion. Ira had spent an afternoon at a gallery studying the paintings of James McNeill Whistler and influenced by Whistler's descriptive titles – Nocturne in Black and Gold, Arrangement in Gray and Black (better known as Whistler's Mother) etc. – why not a Rhapsody in Blue?[3]

> It was Ira, by this time George's best listener, who urged his brother to incorporate the new theme into the work, pointing out to George that its broad lyricism was a good foil to the jazziness of the *Rhapsody*'s first half.[4]

[N.B. Stephen Gilbert has subjected the *Rhapsody* to a Schenkerian analysis in his book *The Music of Gershwin*;[5] I will not replicate that exercise here.]

Tunes into themes

According to all the biographies, Gershwin composed the *Rhapsody* within a few weeks. Ira Gershwin, who claimed more influence over the piece as the years went by, later wrote that he suggested the use of at least one and possibly two pre-existing melodies: the "Glissando" theme and the E-major theme – as well as the name of the piece. The "Train" theme that Gershwin describes is most likely to be the tune played by the trumpets and clarinet at rehearsal 9 – the least-developed theme in the work.

Any Broadway composer had a backlog of tunes waiting for sudden requests: "the trunk." Gershwin may have based all five themes of the *Rhapsody*, as well as the familiar "good evening friends" tag that he may have already turned into "The Man I Love," on songs in his sketch books. I have named the themes to simplify the discussion. The piano plays each theme (except for the "Train" theme) as a solo somewhere in the piece and we can extract these passages as the "germs" of the work (see Ex. 3.1):

Ritornello theme: bars 39 (three before rehearsal 5) to 54
Train theme: bars 91 (rehearsal 9) to 106 (counter-melody only)
Stride theme: bars 181 (rehearsal 19) to 195
Shuffle theme: bars 260 (rehearsal 25) to 296
Love theme: bars 357 (eleven after rehearsal 32) to 382.

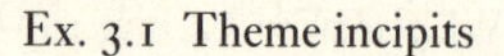

Ex. 3.1 Theme incipits

The five tunes are closely related. They are all based on the "blues scale," with lowered sevenths and major/minor thirds. They all contain the three-note "Man I Love" cell. Three of them contain the same ragtime rhythmic motif (see Ex. 3.2). All five themes imply a 32- (or 16-) bar form. In the *Rhapsody*, none of the themes ends with a clear cadence. Two of the themes (the Ritornello and Shuffle) modulate to a different key from which they began.

Ex. 3.2 Rhythmic motif

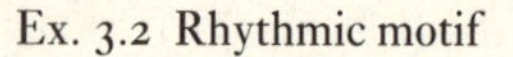

The lack of cadences and the modulating harmonies suggest that even before he began to weave the themes together Gershwin had transformed them from ordinary pop-tune structures. It is not hard to imagine what such models might have sounded like. Example 3.3 contains the five themes of the *Rhapsody* as they appear in the score in their simplest forms, and four hypothetical "trunk" versions. (The "Train" theme is, exceptionally, an unelaborated pop-tune.) Three of the "trunk" tunes are in 16- or 32-bar form; I have imagined trunk song 4 as a 24-bar blues, although it might also be stretched to 32 bars.

(1) "Ritornello" theme (or "Glissando" theme);[6] rehearsal 22–24. This theme is a simple 16-bar AABA in C major with blues-scale melodic inflections. The bridge is in the harmony A flat, the flat sixth,

Ex. 3.3(a) trunk song 1

(b) Ritornello theme

(c) Train theme

(d) trunk song 2

(e) Stride theme
(f) trunk song 3

(g) Shuffle theme

(h) trunk song 4

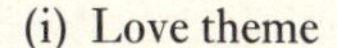

rather than the normal subdominant. In returning to the opening phrase, however, Gershwin treats A flat as if it were the subdominant, so that the closing phrase is no longer in C, but in E flat, up a minor third from the opening. This internal modulation features in every appearance of the Ritornello theme. The versions of the theme heard at the opening of the piece, such as the piano solo at rehearsal 5, stretch the opening phrase to five bars. The choice of A major as the key for the first complete statements of the theme creates a structural link to the other themes: in A major the bridge is built on F, the same harmony as the subdominant bridge sections of the Train and Stride themes which are played in C. Gershwin reharmonizes the Ritornello theme subtly on each appearance. The introductory statement at the very beginning of the work establishes the chromatic voice-leading, avoidance of roots and abundant use of ninth chords which cultivated listeners of the time often associated with Delius. The chromatic inner voices of this harmonic style are so endemic that one resists the impulse to label them thematic; but the *Rhapsody* is anything but "motifless." A four-note chromatic motif appears three times in the first piano solo in rising and falling forms.

The bridge (which Ravel imitated in the first movement of his Piano Concerto in G, see Ex. 3.4) also restates the descending chromatic motif.

(2) "Train" theme; rehearsal 9–11. This comes closest to a simple pop-tune form, a 16-bar AABA in C major. Because the bridge sits on IV, the theme has the harmonic feeling of a simple blues. After the suave harmonizations of the Ritornello, the Train theme has a primitive harmonic cast, but its texture is more complex. Gershwin placed the tune against a rhythmic counter-melody based on the three-note "tag" cell. The counter-melody bears a close resemblance to the main tune of Zez Confrey's "Coaxing the Piano" (see Ex. 3.5); the crossing-hands piano style is pure "novelty piano" *à la* Confrey. Gershwin's theme, however, rearranges Confrey's 2+3+3, as a 3+3+2 pattern; like Confrey Gershwin subdivides the shorter beat into triplet eighth notes. The Train theme also exudes a distinct aroma of klezmer style; with its wailing clarinet and lowered seventh over a pounding additive rhythm it sounds like a *freylakh*. As Bartók's Gershwinesque "Studies on Bulgarian Rhythms" demonstrate, the 3+3+2 additive rhythm of this theme has Eastern European parallels.

(3) "Stride" theme; rehearsal 12–13. This theme shares a tonality and implied structure with the Train theme – AABA' – and might be heard at first as a variant. The last phrase, however, swerves to the dominant

Ex. 3.4 Gershwin: *Rhapsody*; Ravel: Concerto in G

Ex. 3.5 Confrey: "Coaxing the Piano"

save for the climactic statement of the theme at the conclusion of the piece. Gershwin did not make use of the stride-piano style in the piano part of the *Rhapsody*, but if one plays the orchestra's statement of the theme at rehearsal 12 on the piano, its links to stride become obvious. The Prokofiev-like parallel harmonization, however, is not characteristic of stride, but reinforces the "modernistic" element of the work.

(4) "Shuffle" theme; rehearsal 14–16, repeated exactly by the piano from rehearsal 25 to five before 27. This theme contains the most obvious citation of the "Man I Love" tag, as well as the "ragtime" rhythmic motif. The "trunk" prototype is a blues pop-tune similar to "Stairway to Paradise." Gershwin's theme pursues an unexpectedly devious course. It begins in G major, with a 16-bar antecedent phrase, AB, that implies an AC consequent.[7] Instead of rounding out the phrase-group with a consequent, Gershwin makes a sequence up a third from the pattern of the first two bars, then begins the theme again, up another minor third, on the lowered fifth, D flat (with the piano entering with a fragment of the Train theme). The sequential repetition of this modulating structure at the tritone brings the tune back to its original tonic. Gershwin seems to have been proud of his harmonic jugglery; the piano solo at rehearsal 25 is the only extensive near-literal repetition in the work.

(5) "Love" theme; rehearsal 26–32. Over the years this theme has often been likened to the "love" theme from Tchaikovsky's *Romeo and Juliet*; it is also reminiscent of several Rakhmaninov themes written both before and after 1924. (Had his parents stayed in St. Petersburg, Gershwin might have written many such Eastern European blues.) While the other themes of the *Rhapsody* have the self-consciously racy blues character of "Stairway to Paradise," the Love theme would become the model for later and more lyrical Gershwin songs such as "Somebody Loves Me" and "Embraceable You."

The Love theme is the signature of the *Rhapsody*. It is made up of two elements, melody and counter-melody, the first based on the ascending diatonic version of the tag cell, the second on the descending chromatic version. These rich connections to the other themes are hinted at (loudly) by the solo piano just before the cadenza (see Ex. 3.6). The theme is problematic from the standpoints of phrase structure, notation and performance. Its oddity becomes apparent if we compare it with the Berlinesque pop-tune of the "trunk" version. As written for

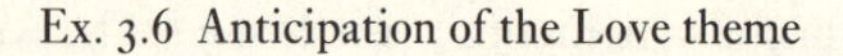

Ex. 3.6 Anticipation of the Love theme

the orchestra at rehearsal 28, Gershwin's theme is a 22-bar long AB antecedent phrase; A consists of two subphrases 8+6, while B is eight bars long. The consequent phrase is exactly parallel until the final cadence – which never arrives, except in the various simplified "song" versions of the sheet music.

Oddly enough, the most famous melody in twentieth-century concert music is never played as written. The theme implies two different possible phrase structures, depending on how the notation is interpreted. On the first Whiteman recording the band plays the Love theme *come scritto*: as an Andantino (slow fox-trot) 8+6+8. Performed in this manner, the counter-melody seems sluggish to our ears. When the piano plays the theme alone, however, Gershwin accelerates during the first four bars of the counter-melody, then ritards in the last two. This change suggests (but avoids) the mechanical tempo relation which has become standard today but which Gershwin never observed: a halving of the tempo of the first two bars of the theme that puffs them up to their full romantic potential. It gives the famous head of the tune a "Grandioso" treatment while restoring the jazzy nervousness of the Confreyesque counter-melody. (Michael Tilson Thomas has told me that Ira Gershwin claimed this, too, was his idea.) This rendition alters the phrase structure of A to 5+4.

There may be two sources of this aporia. If we assume that Gershwin began with an 8+8 model in mind we can see that he stretched out the blues third of the tune. The result *looks* like an eight-bar phrase on the page but *sounds* like an augmentation of a five-bar phrase 2+3. To counteract the augmentation, Gershwin elided the end of A with the beginning of B, making the phrase 8+6. Gershwin's performances show that he intended something different from the way the theme was notated.

He plays it at an erratic tempo with a gradual accelerando. But later performers found a way to play the theme *a tempo* and still retain the jazzy character of the counter-melody. They restored the opening theme to its unaugmented shape by doubling the tempo in the third bar; but the elision of phrases remained, and with it the theme's asymmetry. The variant readings may also reflect a certain confusion over fox-trot notation. Ragtime was usually notated in 2/4. Jazz tunes came to be notated in 4/4. Fox-trots, the transition between the two, were written in 2/4, 4/4 and 2/2. Whiteman interprets this theme as being in a gracious 2/2. In the rhythmic interpretation usually heard today, a broad 4/4 alternates with a hectic 2/2.

(6) The "Man I Love" or "Good Evening Friends" tag was enough of a blues cliché by 1923 that both Gershwin and Milhaud found it irresistible (see Ex. 3.7). The tag appears in overt and covert forms throughout the score. As a four-bar melody it seems to be the property of the piano solo, but it also appears as a three-note cell hidden in the tunes themselves, or as a counter-melody. It appears in many different variants: reorderings, retrogrades, inversions and intervallic diminutions. It has a primary diatonic form of a major second and a minor second, heard in the fifth bar, and a secondary chromatic form of two minor seconds, heard as a counterpoint to the tag at the piano's first entrance (see Ex. 3.8). Once the listener becomes tag-conscious, virtually every bit of "filler" in the score turns out to be thematic.

We can try to distinguish between the overt and covert appearances of the tag, though it is not always easy to do so. With the piano's first entrance the tag appears as a two-bar melodic phrase with an important chromatic counter-melody in the inner voice. With hindsight we see that Gershwin is presenting the diatonic and chromatic forms of the cell simultaneously. The E♮ in the piano is itself worthy of note. It replaces the expected E♭ (against which it sounds in the orchestra) with a chromatic passing tone which also hints at the E major tonality of the Love theme.

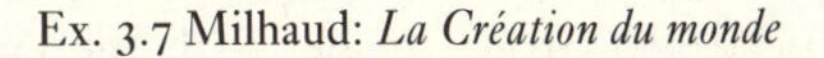
Ex. 3.7 Milhaud: *La Création du monde*

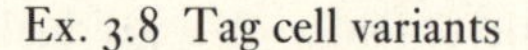
Ex. 3.8 Tag cell variants

If we compare the hypothetical "trunk" originals and actual versions of the themes, we can generalize on how Gershwin transformed self-contained pop-tune material into musical themes even before he began to weave them together. He stretched phrases from four to five bars. He deflected the harmony to push the themes to a tonality a third away from their beginning. He lopped off cadences to make his melodies "endless" – so much so that the Love theme had to have endings written for it by other hands. He made the *Ur*-melodies more dynamic and open-ended, implying regular structures without stating them. He exploited every possible opportunity to glue the themes together with cross-references: a method exposed in the very opening phrase of the work which combines Ritornello and Stride themes with the tag cell. In short, Gershwin worked systematically to prevent the *Rhapsody* from being the simple medley that the work is often taken to be. The weaknesses of the *Rhapsody*, contrary to much criticism, may stem from too much unity, not incoherence – Gershwin could be heavy-handed in his motivic reminders. One anecdote, though, suggests that Gershwin felt that it is harder to write a melody that is not repetitious (like Arlen's "I've Got the World on a String," or Ellington's "In a Sentimental Mood") than a motif-heavy tune like, say, "That Certain Feeling." After Gershwin's death, Arlen wrote: "I can recall an incident when Irving Berlin told a song writer [Arlen] that George had pointed out that this young man's latest effort had demonstrated a particularly original bit of melodic construction in that there was no repetition of phrase from bar to bar in the main theme."[8]

Formal attire

> The *Rhapsody in Blue* remains a quite satisfactory piece. Rhapsodies, however, are not very difficult to write, if one can think up enough tunes.[9]
>
> I've never really studied musical form. That's nothing, of course, to be proud of. But regardless of the kind of music a composer is writing, it must have a definite line of progression. It must have a beginning and an end and a suitable section combining the two, just as the human body, to be complete, must have arms, legs, and a head. In this sense of trying to make my musical compositions each a complete work, I suppose there is a certain form to them.[10]

Although critics have accused the *Rhapsody* of formlessness, it is polymorphous. It exists in many different forms, following divergent functions. In length it ranges from the commercial sound-bite to the quarter of an hour needed to fill a soloist's slot in a symphony concert. Its morphology varies depending on whether it is played as a piano solo, a piece for jazz band, or as a piano concerto, and has also changed with the evolution of recording technology. The present-day orthodoxy of playing the piece in its "complete form" has resulted in a much longer work than Gershwin ever recorded phonographically in his lifetime, or that most listeners heard until well after his death. Despite some obvious *longueurs*, however, the "complete" *Rhapsody* heard today displays a clear formal design:

I: Molto moderato (beginning to rehearsal 9): introductory dialogue between the band and the solo piano leading to two statements of the Ritornello theme, first by the piano, then band, each prefaced by a piano cadenza.

II: Scherzo ABCBB' Trio C.

III: Andante moderato: three statements of the Love theme.

IV: Finale: Piano toccata vamp, followed by rising stretti on the Love theme, leading to climactic statement of the Stride theme. Codetta based on the Ritornello theme and tag.

The *Rhapsody*, at least in its uncut version, is not a rhapsody in the Lisztian sense, but rather a compressed one-movement symphony (like Schoenberg's *Kammersinfonie*, op. 9). Gershwin effectively gave the work a beginning, a middle and an end; the only awkward passages are the apparently underdeveloped Train theme (which functions effectively, however, as a transition to the Stride theme) and the stagnant Trio. The structural intent of the Trio, however, is clear: a cyclic reappearance of the Ritornello theme at the center of the work. Gershwin apparently feared that without this pivotal cross-reference the work would splinter into a mere medley. The actual effect is more interesting, dramatically speaking – when the piano suddenly and grandly restates the opening theme it sounds as though it has lost its way, but then the Trio turns this "memory lapse" into a joke.

The *Rhapsody* when it is played by piano and orchestra is, however, not a symphony but a concerto; and the more detailed formal scheme shows Gershwin's careful solution to the generic problem of who plays what, when and how. After the opening phrase, the piano twice interrupts the band's statements of the Ritornello theme, with a longer solo the second time. Once it has taken command, musically, of center stage, the piano claims the Ritornello for itself with the first complete statement of the theme, followed by an orchestral repetition. The Scherzo shows a similar, but more complicated strategy of transferring the music from the band to the solo. The band plays the Train, Stride and Shuffle themes in rapid succession. The piano then plays its version of the Stride theme, then launches into the Trio, a comic statement of the Ritornello theme stripped of its suave harmonies and five-bar phrases. After a linking passage the piano recapitulates the entire Shuffle theme (compare rehearsals 14 and 25). The three statements of the Love theme seem most straightforward: orchestra, orchestra plus piano counter-melody, piano solo. But, since the theme is built in two parallel phrases with indeterminate endings, the listener may wonder whether there are one-and-a-half statements of a complete ABAC theme, or three statements of an unbalanced antecedent phrase. The piano sets the "finale" in motion with a toccata which becomes a rhythmic descant to the orchestral development of the Love theme. The piano, however, returns to an earlier ploy at rehearsal 37, by recapitulating its first cadenza. This sets up a dramatic surprise: instead of returning to a triumphant statement of the Love theme as the high point, Gershwin uses a *grandioso* statement of the Stride theme – the first time the piano plays this theme rhythmically and in tempo. But Gershwin has two more cards to play. The band brings back the Ritornello (as it was heard at rehearsal 6) in its original key – and the piano then has the last word, a cadenced version of the tag.

In contrasting the piano and the orchestra Gershwin uses two devices: insinuation and character contrast. From its first entry, the piano displays a habit of sneaking in mid-phrase and then moving toward its own statement of a theme – an effective dramatic gesture. Equally theatrical in nature is the composer's use of contrasting affects. The orchestra presents each theme in a single mood; whereas the piano part is full of character indications – *tranquillo*, *agitato*, *poco scherzando*, *brillante*, *espressivo*, *misterioso*, *sognando*, *grandioso* – in short, the full panoply of romantic role-playing familiar from the concerto literature. This strategy gives the soloist a protean, unpredictable and expansive role in the work (helping to overcome the limited technical resources of Gershwin's piano writing) which reaches its apotheosis in the *grandioso* statement of the Stride theme – the one time that a theme from the orchestra is made louder rather than more intimate in its solo statement. This strategy also explains the essential stylistic dualism of the *Rhapsody* – the contrast of a jazz band playing a series of fox-trots with a ruminative and romantic soloist "hero" who transforms the rough jazz materials into an expressive self-portrait by using the musical devices of the "serious" concert world. The most clearly classical and "rhapsodic" elements of the work are the cadenzas and much-criticized connecting passages. Whatever else may be said against them they are crucial to the expressive drama of the music, and they even play a well-planned dramatic and structural role. Most simply, yet seductively, the connecting passages serve to keep the audience waiting for the tunes.

Harmonic structure?

The *Rhapsody*'s harmonic structure would seem to owe little to the classical models Gershwin would have been taught at the conservatory. Critics, bewildered by the many key-changes of the work, have blamed the rambling modulations on Gershwin's lowly experience as a song plugger, where transposition was a necessary trick of the trade. From a conservative academic vantage-point the harmonic organization of the *Rhapsody* certainly would appear unconventional. It begins and ends in the same key, B flat, but this tonal framework is perfunctory, abandoned at the end of the first phrase as the music modulates rapidly in a subdominant direction: B flat, E flat, A flat, D flat, G flat, B, E, finally coming to rest on A major. The ending is similarly brief. The piece appears to be heading towards a final cadence on E flat when the opening phrase suddenly appears in B flat.

It is not hard to find harmonic patterns in the work, however. Gershwin's musical education was based on the romantic piano literature (Chopin, Liszt, Debussy), not the symphonic classics. While the form of the *Rhapsody* is not Lisztian, the harmonic organization appears to follow Lisztian ideals both in large-scale design and smaller details. We know from his scrapbooks that the young Gershwin listened attentively to the Romantic piano and orchestral literature – especially that of the Russian composers who most frequently deployed "symmetrical" harmonic plans and real sequences. How closely Gershwin had studied such examples of Romantic harmony is another question. Modulations based on mediant relations (thirds rather than fifths) were also part of the idiom of Tin Pan Alley. The verse of "Ballin' the Jack" begins with a diminished-seventh sequence, and Gershwin began "I'll Build a Stairway to Paradise" with a similar upward sequence – a half-step ascent that can be found in any book of piano exercises.

In the *Rhapsody* there are strong tonal emphases on B flat, G, E, and C sharp. (The G and C sharp emphases appear as dominant pedals of sections in C and F sharp.) As befits its introductory function, the first part of the piece tumbles through a circle of fifths in the subdominant direction (a kind of structural blues) from B flat, arriving finally at A major, which serves as a Lisztian dominant to the C-major Train theme.

The harmonic deflection within the themes similarly follows Lisztian tendencies: the Ritornello theme modulates up a minor third rather than returning to its tonic, and the G-major Shuffle theme moves upwards by thirds twice so that it can be restated at the tritone, in D flat, and then, by repeating the whole process, return to its opening tonic. Real sequences up and down the whole-tone scale often serve to connect larger tonal functions. Although informed musical taste of the time took Gershwin to task for his hackneyed connective passages, they are a characteristic part of the harmonic idiom of many compositions in which a diminished-seventh chord quadri-tonic takes the place of a simpler hierarchy of keys. Similar sequences in Schumann, Liszt, Wagner and Tchaikovsky help delineate the constant motion of the music beyond the limits of dominant harmony.

Before we hand Gershwin a prize for symmetrical harmony, however, a counter argument needs to be considered. Though a B-flat – G – E – C-sharp tonal framework is present, its proportions are a little odd. If we look at the *Rhapsody* from the middle, from rehearsal 9 to 28, it can seem like a conventional piece in C major with predictable excursions to G (a brief move to A major at rehearsal 20 is the only exception). Despite the harmonic free-fall of the opening, most of the *Rhapsody* is harmonically stable, almost inert. Gershwin even appears to set up an entry of the Love theme in G major, with a huge dramatic half cadence on D at the end of the cadenza, then jumps toward the dominant of E for the Love theme. The substitution of E major for G gives the Love theme its silken sheen, but the evidence of both the *Concerto in F* and the *Second Rhapsody* suggests that Gershwin may have liked E major for such themes no matter what the broader tonal framework. The use of these keys may show Gershwin's determination to set off his most expressive melodies with a harmonic coloring that would separate them clearly from the brittle "jazzy" material that surrounded them, and would allow the string instruments to come to the fore.

4

Ingredients

> Everyone is familiar with the Negro's modification of the white's musical instruments, so that his interpretation has been adopted by the white man himself, and then re-interpreted. In so many words, Paul Whiteman is giving an imitation of a Negro orchestra making use of white-invented instruments in a Negro way. Thus has arisen a new art in the civilized world.[1]

Jazz?

In 1924, New York was the center of American popular music, but it was far from the creative sources of jazz, the deep south, New Orleans, Kansas City and Chicago. Although music called jazz was heard in New York as early as 1915, most jazz histories see the arrival of authentic New Orleans music, and its developments in Chicago, as beginning late in 1924 when Louis Armstrong joined the Fletcher Henderson Band. Bix Beiderbecke and his Wolverines also brought a Chicago version of jazz to New York late in 1924. Recordings by King Oliver's Creole Jazz Band, now considered the greatest exemplar of the New Orleans style, appeared in the summer of 1923, but Oliver did not play in New York until 1927; Jelly Roll Morton similarly did not perform in New York until 1926, after he had made his recordings for Victor.

New York had its own traditions of pre-jazz African-American music largely based in the worlds of social dancing and musical theater. In 1910, James Reese Europe founded the Clef Club, an umbrella organization of black dance orchestras. Beginning with *A Trip to Coontown* in 1897, Bob Cole, Will Marion Cook and Bert Williams composed songs for black musical comedies, a project continued after the war by Noble Sissle, Eubie Blake and James P. Johnson. In the pre-war years African-American musicians dominated the society dancing circuit, and organized themselves as professionals. Many came from a middle-class background and shared the aspirations (and frustrations) of the black bourgeoisie. The New York musical scene was relatively integrated, for its time – which is to say, minimally. Artists might mingle in the piano cubicles at Remick's, but audiences were mostly segregated. Black musicians performed on Broadway and white song writers, like Harold Arlen, composed for the Cotton Club, where blacks performed for a white audience. Will Vodery, a black musician who worked closely with Gershwin, was an arranger for the Ziegfeld Follies. Eubie Blake, James P. Johnson and Fats Waller composed pop-tunes and worked in the same venues as Gershwin. The musical worlds of Harlem and Tin Pan Alley overlapped and influences ran in both directions.

Accounts from the period point to several crucial turns toward "jazz" in New York: in 1912, W. C. Handy published his "Memphis Blues"; in 1915, Vern and Irene Castle popularized the fox-trot, a dance apparently created by James Reese Europe which replaced the jerkiness of ragtime dancing with a more socially respectable elegant glide; in 1916, the Original Dixieland Jazz Band made its first New York appearance. In 1920, the recordings of Mamie Smith launched a blues craze; in 1924, Whiteman performed in Aeolian Hall and Armstrong and Beiderbecke came to New York from Chicago. Each wave demanded a new critical orientation for white listeners, and blacks as well; the Clef Club initially opposed the performances of this vulgar music which threatened its professional standards. Jazz challenged the ideals of vocal production, instrumental technique, intonation, articulation, ensemble and, of course, rhythm. The easiest way to defend the older concepts was to dismiss jazz as "barnyard noise," a commonplace response (also employed against the latest outrages of musical modernism) further fueled by the infamous barnyard effects on the ODJB's performances of "Livery Stable Blues" – with which Whiteman opened his "Experiment."

Early attempts to describe jazz usually reduced it to a few stylistic quirks: there is a common tone of incomprehension and caricature in these rushed formulations, but also evidence that anyone claiming to be a musical sophisticate had to weigh in on the subject. Charles Welton, writing about Europe's band for the New York *World* in 1919, claimed that "the basic fundamentals of jazz . . . are created by means of a variety of cones inserted point down in the bells of the horns."[2] Others cited the glissando as the defining feature of jazz: "Portamento effects on wind instruments are the real jazz."[3] Writing in the *American Mercury* in 1924 Virgil Thomson reduced it to a rhythmic formula: "Jazz in brief is a compound of (a) the fox-trot rhythm, a four-four measure (alla breve) [*sic*] with a double accent, and (b) a syncopated melody over this rhythm."[4] Aaron Copland, writing for the more technically sophisticated readership of *Modern Music* in 1927, claimed that "polyrhythm is the real contribution of jazz"; he defined polyrhythm as the conflict of a "rhythm of four quarters split into eight eighths . . . arranged thus: 1–2–3:1–2–3–4–5, or even more precisely: 1–2–3:1–2–3:1–2."[5] Such a formula describes ragtime and novelty pieces and Copland's own music, but little of, say, Louis Armstrong's music of the time. However, Copland's writings, like Thomson's, provide scant evidence that they actually listened to jazz. Strangely, neither Thomson nor Copland mentions the "blue note" which for many others represented the definitive marker of jazz; Thomson identifies a "blues formula" ("subdominant modulation with alternations of tonic major and minor") and refers to the assimilation of standard "advanced" harmonies, such as augmented-sixth chords "in a manner that is not at all crude." Jazz "authority" Henry Osgood made fun of these reductionist views as early as 1926: yet Gershwin and Grofé deployed all of these devices – mutes, glissandi, fox-trot rhythms, 3+3+2 rhythms, blue notes, subdominant modulations and augmented-sixth chords – conspicuously and systematically in *Rhapsody in Blue*.

The fox-trot and James Reese Europe

> One day, during the same period, while roller-skating in Harlem, he heard jazz music outside the Baron Wilkins Club where Jim Europe and his band performed regularly. The exciting rhythms and raucous tunes made such an impression on him that he never forgot them. From then on he often skated up to the club and sat down on the sidewalk outside to listen to the music. He later told a friend that his lifelong fascination for Negro rags, blues and spirituals undoubtedly began at this time; that Jim Europe's music was partially responsible for his writing works like *135th Street* and parts of *Porgy and Bess*.[6]

On 11 March, 1914, James Reese Europe led the Clef Club Orchestra in a concert at Carnegie Hall; the orchestra consisted of 47 mandolins, 27 harp-guitars, 11 banjos, 8 violins, 1 saxophone, 1 tuba, 13 cellos, 2 clarinets, 2 baritone horns, 8 trombones, 7 cornets, 1 set of timpani, 5 traps and 2 string basses.[7] Though the concert sounds like a precursor of Whiteman's 1924 "Experiment," it was presented as a demonstration of African-American culture and not, as in Whiteman's case, as an example of "modern" music. Unfortunately no recordings of this concert exist, though a re-creation by Maurice Peress was performed in New York in 1989. Europe returned to Carnegie Hall in 1914 with the National Negro Symphony Orchestra for a program mainly of spirituals and "plantation songs," which the critics applauded, and more recent popular numbers like J. Rosamond Johnson's "Under the Bamboo Tree," which one critic dismissed as a vulgar imitation of Tin Pan Alley.[8] Apparently the familiar religious and sentimental genres of black music were less threatening than the emerging popular forms. Though the Carnegie Hall concerts attracted considerable attention, Europe achieved even greater fame as musical director for Irene and Vernon Castle, and inventor, in 1915, of the fox-trot. Europe claimed that he found the source of the fox-trot in the rhythms of W. C. Handy's "Memphis Blues."[9] While Europe emphasized the origins of the fox-trot in African-American dance, the success of the step, which was to become the twentieth-century equivalent of the minuet, stemmed from its combination of eroticism and genteel elegance. Couples could now dance "cheek to cheek," but they were commanded to move with refinement: "Do not wriggle the shoulders. Do not shake the hips. Do not twist the body. Do not flounce the elbows. Do not pump the arm. Do not hop – glide instead. Avoid low, fantastic and acrobatic dips. . . . Drop the Turkey Trot, the Grizzly Bear, the Bunny Hug, etc. These dances are ugly, ungraceful and out of fashion."[10] The rhythmic novelty of the step was its slowed tempo. Vernon Castle told the *Ladies Home Journal*: "If you will play an ordinary "rag" half as fast as you would play it for the one-step you will have a pretty good idea of the music and tempo."[11] The arrival of the fox-trot was manifest in music by a change from notation in 2/4 time to 4/4 or 2/2 – often with identical musical results. The confusion over tempo and notation shows up clearly, and still problematically, in the score of *Rhapsody in Blue*, most notably in its E-major theme.

Piano styles

By the time he was twenty Gershwin had encountered many different styles of piano playing. Aside from classical piano, which he studied seriously (if sporadically) for eight years, Gershwin drew on several post-ragtime idioms, the song-plugger style of Les Copeland and Mike Bernard, the stride-piano style of Luckey Roberts and James P. Johnson, the novelty piano of Felix Arndt, Zez Confrey, Victor Arden and Phil Ohman, and the comic piano of Chico Marx and Jimmy Durante. We can differentiate these styles as follows.

Song-plugger piano: the genre was a form of advertising. Song pluggers introduced the latest tunes at cabarets to promote sheet-music sales. To make the greatest possible impression, the song plugger had to create the illusion of a singer accompanied by an orchestra. The orchestral effect was heightened on piano rolls, which could go beyond the limits of a player's ten fingers. The evidence of Gershwin's *Songbook* and of his recording and piano rolls suggests that he thought of these songs-without-words as fixed compositions which he honed and perfected at first for song plugging and later for entertainment at parties. The structure follows a song closely, usually with both verse and chorus. The melody often appears as a middle voice, to keep it in an easily sung register. The pianist surrounds the melody with figuration derived from ragtime or classical music. In the preface to his *Songbook*, Gershwin advised pianists that the style of performance should be unclassical, staccato rather than legato and with little use of pedal.

Stride piano: Although it shares some stylistic features with song-plugger piano, stride had a different social function and was exclusively played by African-American pianists. Stride piano, as Paul Machlin notes:

> originated to a large extent in the social milieu of Harlem's informal nightlife – specifically, at rent parties. . . . The pianist's major responsibility at these affairs was to insure that the music, proceeding continuously, facilitated constant dancing. . . . In order to keep the music fresh and vital, and to keep the dancers' energy from flagging, improvisation became a practical as well as aesthetic necessity.[12]

Stride compositions like James P. Johnson's "Carolina Shout" served as severe tests of an aspirant's skill. The music was virtuosic and rhythmic, though not particularly melodic. The left hand took the place of a rhythm section. Stride pianists replaced the octaves of ragtime with tenths and rolled chords, and made surprising alterations in accent within the bar. They added sevenths, ninths and blue notes to the triadic harmonies of ragtime. Although many stride compositions were published and performed as written, the repetitions of musical sections were usually varied, and in performance the stride masters mixed composed and improvised elements in order to stretch out a piece almost infinitely.

Novelty piano: a late ragtime style developed mainly in the Midwest for classically trained amateurs who wanted to play syncopated music, though it was also performed by specialists like Confrey or the team of Arden and Ohman (who appeared in Gershwin's *Lady be Good* in 1924). It follows the form of ragtime but with greater rhythmic complexity and harmonic sophistication. The music is full of intricate cross-rhythms, produced by grouping eighth notes in threes rather than twos, and the harmony is "modernistic," full of "Chinese" parallel fourths and "Impressionist" parallel ninth chords, but also alludes to the blues. Confrey's famous "Kitten on the Keys" of 1921 displays all of these traits (see Ex. 4.1). In the twenties, novelty piano was the harbinger of symphonic jazz, and Confrey was taken to be at least as important a contributor to the form as Whiteman. Confreyisms abound in Gershwin's piano solos and even in Copland's.

Comic piano: a vaudeville style which burlesqued both classical and ragtime music. Unlike novelty piano it was often played in a *scherzando* mood with hesitations to set up the comic effects similar to novelty piano. Chico Marx and Jimmy Durante were the main exponents.

These piano styles overlapped. Gershwin and the stride pianists were well aware of each other; Gershwin paid frequent late-night visits to Harlem cabarets to hear them in their element; downtown, in high society, they often performed at the same parties. Gershwin, Confrey, Johnson, Waller and later Art Tatum, the ultimate stride master, all shared an interest in classical music of the parlor variety. Confrey published a novelty version of Rubinstein's *Melody in F*, as well as Mendelssohn's

Ex. 4.1 Confrey: "Kitten on the Keys"

"Spring Song" and Schumann's "Träumerei." Tatum often performed an extravagant version of Massenet's "Elegie," much to the displeasure of jazz purists. Waller recorded many songs in a style modeled closely on Gershwin's song-plugger manner: Johnson and Waller composed piano "novelties" in the style of Confrey. The novelty genre could also be extended to include Gershwin's *Preludes* and Copland's *Piano Blues*.

Traces of all four styles can be found in the *Rhapsody*, though some are more apparent in the orchestral material than in the solo piano part. Song-plugger versions of three of the main themes appear two bars before rehearsal 5 (Ritornello theme), rehearsal 25 (Shuffle theme) and rehearsal 32 (Love theme). Stride piano is heard in the orchestra at rehearsal 12 (Stride theme) (compare this passage with Johnson's "Snowy Mornin' Blues" (see Ex. 4.2). Novelty piano is heard at rehearsal 9 (Train theme) and in many of the two-handed arpeggio figures. Comic piano *à la* Chico Marx appears at rehearsal 22.

Once we have identified these styles, however, it becomes clear how much of the *Rhapsody* is written in a style that is different from any of them, and especially different from Gershwin's well-documented song-plugger manner. Most of the *Rhapsody*'s solo part is in a pop-romantic cadenza style recognizable in Gershwin's three other works for piano and orchestra. It sounds generically like late nineteenth-century classical piano writing, somewhere between Tchaikovsky and Grieg, with a few

Ex. 4.2 J. P. Johnson: "Snowy Mornin' Blues"

hints of early Debussy, though only occasionally is it reminiscent of specific pieces. Most noticeably unjazz-like is the rubato performance style of all the large piano solos, and the use of classical character types such as *agitato*, *sognando* and *scherzando* in the solo piano's reinterpretation of the thematic material. A similar "art" style appears in some of Confrey's works, such as the "Three Little Oddities" of 1923 and the "Fantasy (Classical)" of 1926 which comes with a "jazz" variation.

"Modernistic" music

Just as European classical composers began to imitate jazz, popular composers absorbed aspects of modern harmony into their music. An entire genre called "modernistic" grew out of this. Closely related to novelty piano, the genre includes works by James P. Johnson ("You've Got to be Modernistic"), Jelly Roll Morton ("Freakish"), Zez Confrey ("Champagne"), Bix Beiderbecke ("In a Mist"), Don Redman ("Chant of the Weed") and Coleman Hawkins ("Queer Notions"). The term "modernistic" carried two related kinds of association, the Orient and drugs, both of which tied it, loosely, to Impressionism. (In jazz the modernistic genre spawned a subgenre of "reefer" music.) Impressionist devices such as parallel fourths, fifths and triads, dominant-ninth chords and whole-tone scales are markers of the style. Most often the modernistic devices call attention to themselves in a harmonic context which is still close to ragtime.

It is questionable to what extent "modernistic" music was based on contact with actual pieces of modern music. The technical devices associated with the modernistic genre seem to have a life of their own. Self-conscious allusions to modernist masterpieces did not appear in jazz until the late forties, with the obligatory quotes from *Petrushka* or *Le sacre du printemps* in bebop solos, or Stan Kenton's echoes of *Daphnis et Chloé*. At the time of the *Rhapsody*, Gershwin, however, may have been familiar with some of Debussy's piano music.[13] Compare bar 55 of the *Rhapsody* with bars 30–31 of the Toccata from *Pour le piano*, and bar 68 of the *Rhapsody* with the figure from bar 32 of *Reflets dans l'eau* (see Ex. 4.3). Gershwin's later music expanded the devices of modernism to include Stravinskian polychords (and Poulencian insouciance) in *An American in Paris* and even Schoenbergian twelve-tone figures in the *"I Got Rhythm" Variations* and *Porgy and Bess* (where the harmony often sounds like Berg's). These more advanced modernisms did not enter jazz usage until the late forties with Ellington's nearly atonal *Clothed Woman* and the "progressive jazz" of the Kenton Orchestra; progressive jazz was a mutation of "modernism."

Ex. 4.3(a) Gershwin: *Rhapsody*, b. 55; Debussy: *Pour le piano*, bb. 30–31;
(b) Gershwin: *Rhapsody*, b. 68; Debussy: *Reflets dans L'eau*, b. 32

Popular song and the blues

The modern American popular song emerged just before the First World War.[14] Few songs written before "Alexander's Ragtime Band" became part of the canon that dominated American popular culture until the rise of rock. Gershwin acknowledged three predecessors – Berlin, Kern and Handy – and each of these figures represented larger musical traditions. Berlin saw himself as a reborn Stephen Foster, and also as the heir to George M. Cohan. Kern mediated between the worlds of musical comedy and operetta. Gershwin wrote that "Kern was the first composer who made me conscious that most popular music was of inferior quality and that musical comedy was made of better material."[15] Handy was the self-styled "Father of the Blues." According to Joan Peyser, Gershwin gave Handy a first edition of the score of the *Rhapsody* inscribed "to Mr. Handy, whose early blues songs are the forefathers of this work."[16]

Gershwin's early songs, many of which are modeled on hits by Berlin, Kern and Handy, bear out his "great man" model for pop-tune history. But the most influential popular songs of the teens were composed mainly by largely forgotten African-Americans. The process of "forgetting" began as early as Isaac Goldberg's *Tin Pan Alley* of 1930, which makes no mention of these songs. Irving Berlin had also clouded the picture by claiming that American popular song was created by composers "of Russian birth and ancestry" and "of pure white blood."[17] The invisibility of many of the authors, however, is a key to the role the songs played in the evolution of the popular idiom. They were a bridge between racially stereotyped "coon" songs and racially neutral, or ambiguous, pop-tunes, a process begun, according to Alec Wilder, by "You Been a Good Old Wagon, But You Done Broke Down" written in 1895 by Ben Harney, a black who passed for white (at least according to Eubie Blake). The hit songs of 1910–20 allowed the rhythms and inflections of African-American music to pass for "American." In his essential *History of the Blues*, Francis Davis draws attention to these popular songs as models for the blues songs of Cohan, Berlin and Gershwin:[18]

"Ballin' the Jack"	Chris Smith and Jim Burris
"Some of these Days"	Shelton Brooks
"I Aint Got Nobody"	Spencer Williams
"Pretty Baby"	Tony Jackson
"If I Could Be With You One Hour Tonight"	J. P. Johnson
"After You've Gone'	J. Turner Layton and Henry Creamer
"Way Down Yonder in New Orleans"	Layton and Creamer
"I'm Just Wild about Harry"	Eubie Blake
"Sweet Georgia Brown"	Maceo Parker, Ben Bernie and Kenneth Casey
"I'm Coming Virginia"	Will Marion Cook
"A Good Man is Hard to Find"	Eddie Green

to which Alec Wilder adds:[19]

"The Darktown Strutters Ball"	Shelton Brooks
"Waiting for the Robert E. Lee"	Lewis Muir
"My Melancholy Baby"	Ernie Burnett
"Poor Butterfly"	Raymond Hubbell
"For Me and My Gal"	George Meyer
"Ja-Da"	Bob Carleton
"Baby Won't You Please Come Home"	Charles Warfield and Clarence Williams
"There'll be Some Changes Made"	W. Benton Overstreet

These songs were mostly free of the stereotypical codewords and props that marked the older "coon" songs, whether written by blacks or whites; they were also free of the Celtic sentimentality that persisted in Cohan's songs and other popular hits of the period. They established a new rhythm for the entire American language, not for just a few dialects.

The style of these "transitional" popular songs helps put in perspective Gershwin's use of the blues. At the time of the *Rhapsody* the blues had a double identity, at least as far as the music industry was concerned. We might term these "pop" blues and "race" blues.[20] The first took the form of published popular songs, most notably Handy's "St. Louis Blues" of 1914 (the most often recorded song in America between1900 and 1950).[21] The second blues genre appeared on records, beginning with Mamie Smith's "Crazy Blues" of 1920. These were performed by women and aimed at a black audience, although whites bought them too. As Francis Davis notes, the term "race" as applied to these records had a double meaning: for blacks it meant "ours"; for whites, "raciness."[22] Interestingly, in this period jazz recordings were not sold on "race labels." Jazz had a much larger white audience than did the blues, at least in its "race" versions. Gershwin, like most of the tunesmiths, was highly influenced by Handy's published pop blues. In his music of the twenties there is little evidence of the influence of "race" records other than an element of raciness which leapt to the public's attention in "I'll Build a Stairway to Paradise" in 1922.

W. C. Handy's *Blues: an Anthology*, published in 1926, contains both traditional blues and recent blues compositions by Handy and others; it put the blues within the reach of any American family with a piano. His "St. Louis Blues," a three-part hybrid of blues and tango, changed the landscape of American music almost from its appearance in 1914. Whether Handy was a transcriber or composer, arranging the blues for piano was already a significant act of acculturation. The blues was guitar-based, and blues harmony exploited the guitar's ability to bend pitch. Handy had to find ways of reconciling the blues with the tempered scale of the piano. "Memphis Blues," while rarely going beyond the confines of hymnbook harmony, employs accented neighbor tones, acciaccaturas and clashing tones to simulate blue notes on the piano – devices still in use today. Gershwin rarely composed in the blues form, and never for blues singers, but Handy's published blues served him as an anthology of blues formulas which could be incorporated into the pop-tune format.

Gershwin's stylistic development to 1923

Gershwin's style took form most clearly in the following songs written before the *Rhapsody*.

"I Was So Young (You Were So Beautiful)" (1919); lyrics by Irving Caesar and Alfred Bryan. This early song almost sounds like mature Gershwin; the opening bars of the chorus prefigure the Love theme of the *Rhapsody* (see Ex. 4.4). This four-bar phrase sounds so fresh that the hackneyed quality of the next four bars, with their awkward tritone leap, comes as a jolt. But the second half of the chorus is even more of a surprise. Gershwin implies a simple ABAC 4+4+4+4 design but stretches C to ten bars by developing the first three notes of the melody as a motif. Instead of feeling pedantic the insistence on this motif gives the song an intimate, amorous quality, which Gershwin must have remembered when he composed the *Rhapsody*.

"Swanee" (1919); lyrics by Irving Caesar. Al Jolson served to make this song Gershwin's first hit; and like Jolson it sounds as though it comes from an earlier era of blackface – or perhaps it is intended as a parody of the style. The verse is unusual: almost a self-contained song, it is in the parallel minor to the chorus. But at the second phrase, Gershwin unexpectedly suggests the Dorian mode by using the major-sixth degree (see Ex. 4.5). The effect is both startling and expressive, and takes the song beyond the boundaries of its genre. In the chorus Gershwin exploits the raised fifth systematically. It first appears in the tenor, then moves to the melody where it becomes the crux of melodic

Ex. 4.4 Gershwin: "I was so young"

Ex. 4.5 Gershwin: "Swanee"

movement. The fact that this pitch is the one that Gershwin avoided in the verse is sophisticated to say the least.

"Nobody but You" (1919); lyrics by Arthur Jackson and B. G. De Sylva. This simple fox-trot was one of the few early songs that Gershwin included in his *Songbook* (1930). Its stepwise melodic line and harmonic progression are very close to "But Not For Me," also of 1930. Its simplicity is the key to its freshness. The melody of the chorus is completely diatonic, inflected by carefully limited chromaticism in the accompaniment.

"Boy Wanted" (1921); lyrics by "Arthur Francis" (Ira Gershwin). The fourth stanza is a give-away to the author's identity: "The movies he must avoid; he'll know his Nietzsche and Freud. I said a boy wanted, one who knows books / Boy wanted, needn't have looks." Again the simplicity of this song is its essence. It is a rhythm song, but lighter than "Swanee." The syncopation of the melody barely calls attention to itself, yet it keeps the voice off the downbeat. The song only becomes arty in its closing C section, which is stretched to sixteen bars and ends on an untypical, theatrical high note.

"Do It Again" (1922); lyrics by B. G. De Sylva. A classic fox-trot, perhaps the model for the one in Ravel's *L'Enfant et les sortilèges*. Rhythmically the chorus displays the double metric scheme essential to the fox-trot: the melody is in a slow two, while the accompaniment bounces along in four. The carping repeated notes of the verse are a set-up for their transformation for the "no, no, no, no, no" in the chorus. But the song stands out for a simple harmonic device. As in "Nobody But You," the melody is based on a scale, but in this case it is the D minor blues scale: D E F F♯ G A B♭ C. While the melody emphasizes the tonic and dominant of this scale, the harmony places the song in F major. The song does not sound polytonal (though it may have suggested the idea of a bitonal fox-trot to Ravel), but it is composed on bitonal principals. (Oscar Levant described the song as "Frenchy.") The rhythmic manipulation of the "do it again" motif shows to advantage Gershwin's ever-greater melodic precision.[23]

"I'll Build a Stairway to Paradise" (1922); lyrics by B. G. De Sylva and Ira Gershwin. The song was the sensation of George White's *Scandals of 1922*, which featured the Paul Whiteman Band, and of Eva Gauthier's November 1923 song recital. Basically it is just another dance-step plugging number. The verse steals shamelessly from "Ballin' the Jack," but compounds its chromaticism (see Ex. 4.6) Gershwin moves his melody up a half-step every two bars, then starts the process over again at the minor third. The chorus, by contrast, is a 16-bar blues, or rather a hybrid blues pop-tune in AA'BA" form. The overt bluesiness of the song was considered sensational at the time; but what was really new was the combination of the blues scale with Broadway sassiness; the lyrics of the song have nothing to do with the blues.[24] The song has an air of self-conscious novelty about it. Wilder finds it "stiffly contrived and synthetic",[25] words which might also be applied to parts of the *Rhapsody*.

Blue Monday

By 1922, Gershwin had defined the elements of his style and begun a synthesis; all that remained was an attempt at larger classical forms. His first try, *Blue Monday*, was ambitious, but a disaster.[26] This one-act "jazz" opera, orchestrated by Will Vodery, had a single staged performance in the *Scandals of 1922*. The action is a ridiculous piece of *verismo*, Pagliacci on 135th Street, and although the characters are black we could just as easily be in Naples or in the Yiddish theaters of the Lower East Side. It is still hard to tell if it was meant to be taken straight, or as a parody. Most of the critics howled with derision: "It is the most dismal, stupid and incredible black-face sketch that has probably

Ex. 4.6 Chris Smith: "Ballin' the Jack" verse; Gershwin: "Stairway to Paradise"

ever been perpetuated," wrote Charles Darnton in the *World*.[27] With the appearance of black musicals like *Shuffle Along* and the emergence of black stars such as Paul Robeson and Ethel Waters, the minstrel convention of blackface, which survived in the vastly popular performances of Al Jolson and Eddie Cantor, had become an embarrassment – at least to some critics. It is hard to tell from the reviews, though, whether critics found the Harlem setting itself offensive, or whether they were put off by Gershwin and De Sylva's crude treatment of it. The published score shows many signs of sanitization; a recent recording drops all derogatory racial references from the lyrics.[28] The work still seems awkward, naïve and dramatically inept, but we should remember that Gershwin had not yet composed a complete musical; he was still a song writer with little dramatic experience. Whiteman gave *Blue Monday* a concert performance in 1925 with a new jazzier scoring by Grofé, which did not improve its critical reception.[29]

Yet *Blue Monday* shows intriguing connections to the *Rhapsody* in its construction. It is built around three songs: "Blue Monday Blues," a blues-scale pop-tune that concludes with a phrase that will become the "Man I Love" tag of the *Rhapsody*; "Has Anyone Seen My Joe," an E-major love theme (!) derived from Gershwin's *Lullaby* for string quartet, written in 1919, and vaguely reminiscent of Albeniz's *Tango*; and finally a pseudo-spiritual, "I'm Going to see my Mother," obviously beholden to "Old Black Joe." Gershwin ties these together with a "tag" motif, just as in the *Rhapsody*. He also makes frequent use of modulating sequences up a third, for instance at the very opening of the opera. As in the *Rhapsody*, Gershwin evokes classical practice by suspending the regular beat. In *Blue Monday* the classical moments are "recitatives"; in the *Rhapsody* they are cadenzas. And as in the *Rhapsody* these classical devices seem to be drawn from a generic notion of the classics rather than from actual works. *Blue Monday* gives no evidence that Gershwin (or De Sylva) had ever seen an opera, but Italian opera belonged as much to the world of popular culture as to the opera house, as the (intentional) travesties by the Marx Brothers and Sid Caesar would show.

Gershwin and the classics

Gershwin studied classical piano formally (though never full time) from 1910 to 1918, when his teacher Charles Hambitzer died in the flu epidemic. He never recorded any classical piano pieces, and his compositions are remarkably free of classical echoes. When he was commissioned to compose a concerto he said that he looked up the form in a musical dictionary – evidence (if it is true) that he never encountered the concerto literature as a player. According to legend, he was first attracted to classical music at the age of six: "I stood outside a penny arcade [on 125th Street] listening to an automatic piano leaping through Rubinstein's Melody in F. The peculiar jumps in the music held me rooted."[30] At the age of ten, he heard Dvořák's "Humoresque" played on the violin by a classmate at P.S. 25. It is also said that Gershwin could play the piano even before his family acquired one in 1910; he soon could play the *William Tell* Overture – though in what arrangement is not clear. He began studies with Hambitzer in 1912 and started keeping a musical scrapbook, mainly filled with clippings from *The Etude*. According to

Goldberg, he pasted in pictures of Liszt, Hofmann, Bauer, Busoni, Bloomfield-Zeisler and Levinne, as well as stories about Russian composers. Hambitzer introduced Gershwin to the music of Liszt, Chopin and Debussy, and made Gershwin "harmony conscious."[31] After Hambitzer's death Gershwin studied harmony, counterpoint and orchestration with Edward Kilenyi for two years, while he was busy as a song plugger and composer. Charles Schwartz has written that the Kilenyi notebooks reveal that Gershwin's harmony lessons were of the most elementary kind, and "do not suggest that Gershwin had any experience with the intricacies of late nineteenth-century chromatic harmony."[32] Later he studied very briefly with Rubin Goldmark.

It is clear that Gershwin's musical education was haphazard at best; but that classical music was undoubtedly part of Gershwin's cultural birthright: classics were played in arcades and schoolyards; reputable teachers could be found even in rough neighborhoods; libraries and concert halls were a subway ride away. Gershwin liked to present himself, especially to other composers, as a primitive, but it was a half-truth. While he never developed the technique to be a classical pianist, and never received the kind of intense academic training Boulanger would give young Americans in Paris, he was a voracious listener in a city that was full of music, and would continue to seek out new musical experiences all his life – whether in going to hear the New York première of *Wozzeck* in 1931 or seeking out the young Art Tatum.

Gershwin absorbed the classics on his own terms. He kept them at a distance – listening but not memorizing, studying but not mastering. It is as though if he knew that he had to defend himself against their influence in order to preserve his own originality.

Whiteman, Grofé: symphonic jazz

> The Man in the Street gained his knowledge of jazz from the symphonic perversions of Paul Whiteman which, in attempting to make jazz respectable, deprived it of all validity. The soaring strings souped up the texture, the chromatic sequences inflated the feeling, the bulging brass elephantized the sonority, until the result was an exact equivalent for the "substitute living" of the worst aspects of Hollywood.[33]

> Excellent intonation, perfect balances, and clean attacks do not necessarily equate with superficiality. There is in the best Whiteman performances a feeling and a personal sound as unique in its way as Ellington's or Basie's. It was just not based on a jazz conception.[34]

Paul Whiteman, once the King of Jazz, seems to be emerging from the reputation of being the "most maligned figure in jazz history," as Gunther Schuller termed him;[35] even his surname has been held against him. Yet as the extracts above indicate, he remains controversial. Disparagement of Whiteman, and a sense that his was a less-than-authentic version of the real jazz, may be traced to Darius Milhaud:

> The jazz orchestra of the Hotel Brunswick was conducted by a young violinist called Reissmann [Leo Reisman? A white violinist who was the leader of the "string quartet of dance orchestras" and was a friend of Gershwin's]. . . . It made a contrast to Paul Whiteman's lively orchestra, which I had heard a few days before in New York and which had the precision of an elegant, well-oiled machine, a sort of Rolls-Royce of dance music, but whose atmosphere remained entirely of the world.[36]

Milhaud's comparison, which was made retrospectively in the late forties, is not necessarily a put-down; on recordings the Whiteman band still sounds like a Rolls-Royce. Unfortunately, most reconstructions of Whiteman's charts sound like an old Chevy.

To white observers of the period, even those familiar with African-American music, there was no doubt that Whiteman's band was representative of jazz. Olin Downes, in his review of the Aeolian Hall concert, captured the exotic impact of the band's performances:

> They have a technic of their own. They play with an abandon equalled only by that race of born musicians – the American Negro, who has surely contributed fundamentally to this art which can neither be frowned nor sneered away. They did not play like an army going through ordered manoeuvres, but like the melomaniacs they are, bitten by rhythms that would have twiddled the toes of St. Anthony.[37]

Writing in 1926, Henry Osgood made the claim that Ferde Grofé, who began to work with Whiteman in 1920, was "the father of modern jazz instrumentation."[38] Like Whiteman, Grofé was the rebellious son of classical musicians; both men moved West to get away from their families. According to Collier, some time after 1914 Grofé began to work with a San Francisco dance band led by Art Hickman: "It may have been Hickman who decided to build his band around a choir of saxophones, novelty instruments then having a considerable vogue, but it was undoubtedly Grofé who worked out the system of playing off other instruments in the orchestra against the saxophones in a vaguely contrapuntal fashion."[39] Grofé brought this system to Whiteman, and created Whiteman's first hits – "Whispering," "Japanese Sandman" and "Avalon" – in 1920. Whiteman soon began to refer to this method of scoring as "symphonic jazz." It was an eye-catching phrase in an era that was also witnessing the birth of many "jazz symphonies."

Gunther Schuller's claim that the Whiteman band lacked a jazz conception is somewhat anachronistic, at least at the time of the "Experiment," when Whiteman's band differed little in its style of jazz performances from that heard on many of the tracks recorded by the Fletcher Henderson Orchestra prior to Armstrong's arrival. The main difference in early 1924 was the far greater complexity of Whiteman's arrangements, the breadth of the Whiteman repertory and the polish of Whiteman's performances (a quality often viewed by jazz critics with suspicion even when it appears in bands, like Lunceford's, with impeccable jazz credentials).

To understand the impact of the "Experiment," however, we need to get beyond the polemics and listen to Whiteman's Band. Considering how much Whiteman recorded there is surprisingly little available today, and the "hipper" record shops refuse to put them in the jazz section. There is a fine British Whiteman anthology on Pavilion Records, produced by Stuart Upton.[40] It contains selections from 1921 to 1934 including "South Sea Island," an early Gershwin tune, and Victor Herbert's *Suite of Serenades*. The collection does not give a good representation of jazz performances by the Whiteman Band: there are no tracks with Trumbauer or Beiderbecke, such as the classic "Changes," and only one with Bing Crosby and the Rhythm Boys. But this emphasis on non-jazz repertory reflects the balance of the band's repertory. It was not a jazz band, but a pops-and-dance band. There are smooth renditions of pop-tunes like "Southern Rose", "I'm a Dreamer" and "It All Depends on You"; skillful renditions of light classics such as "The Parade of the Tin Soldiers" and Herbert's *Suite*; and modernistic confections such as Grofé's "Three Shades of Blue," Peter DeRose's "Deep Purple," and

Matt Malneck's "Caprice Futuristic" and "Park Avenue Fantasy".[41] The eminently danceable, if not swinging, fox-trots were probably most typical of the band in its early years; they are also close enough to the jazz of the time to be confused with it. The increasingly pretentious modernistic numbers of the later years sound like attempts to recapture the glory that was *Rhapsody in Blue*. They remix the same ingredients of jazz (slightly updated), modernist harmonies and lush romantic melodies. "Deep Purple" reduced the *Rhapsody* to camp – and became a national hit. Although there are a number of remarkable instrumental solos, most notably Wilbur Hall's trombone pyrotechnics on "Nola," there are no jazz solos among these tracks. Indeed, very little of this repertory is related to jazz. But all of it is played with an unfailing precision and stylishness.

Whiteman provided a model of cultural synthesis, or at least musical homogenization. At its worst this approach trivialized everything it touched; at its best it expanded the range of musical experiences available to an unsophisticated mass audience. For many listeners, Whiteman's music opened the door to jazz and to the classics. But taken in large doses the slickness begins to pall. The recorded Whiteman legacy is interesting as an archive of superb performances of forgettable music – with one big exception.

5

Inception: the Aeolian Hall concert

> Thus the Livery Stable Blues was introduced apologetically as an example of the depraved past from which modern jazz has risen. The apology is herewith indignantly rejected, for this is a glorious piece of impudence, much better in its unbuttoned jocosity and Rabelaisian laughter than other and more polite compositions that came later.[1]

> It is common gossip on Broadway that between Paul Whiteman and George Gershwin exists a friendly feud as to who made whom.[2]

Seventy years after the event, the artistic motives behind Whiteman's "Experiment in Modern Music" remain obscure. The program was hardly experimental. Aside from Gershwin's *Rhapsody*, it consisted of entirely familiar material, the only innovation being its concert-hall setting. It clearly was not modern music of the kind that New Yorkers had only recently heard. Critics were still reeling from the local premières of *Le sacre du printemps*, *Herzgewächse* and *Octandre*. Most of Whiteman's concert consisted of a series of fox-trots which the band could have played in its usual dance-hall setting. This normal stylistic range was only slightly broadened by the presence of a couple of comedy numbers and Victor Herbert's *Suite of Serenades*, a new work based on old materials by a composer who was already old-fashioned. The concert seems in retrospect to have been a pretentious showcase for a successful dance band. Yet the audience, much of which was drawn from the world of classical music, and many of the critics as well, took a good deal of it seriously. They wanted to believe the fact – or at least entertain the notion – that there was an alternative modern music to the outrages of, say, Varèse, who according to one critic caused "peaceful lovers of music to scream out their agony, to arouse angry emotion and tempt men to retire to the back of the theater and perform tympanal concertos on each other's faces."[3] The audience perhaps suspected that jazz might offer an alternative to the musical vanguard, but it seemed confused about what actually constituted jazz and what elements in this novel music – which gave its name to the era – contributed to its vital appeal.

Attributes of jazz which later critics consider essential to its identity and development, such as improvisation and the blues, and even swing, were not as clearly evident in 1924 as they would be a few years later – largely through the innovative and influential playing of Louis Armstrong. Much of the repertory played by jazz bands and stride pianists in New York at the time was fully composed and based on ragtime, not the blues. Even the saxophone had not yet attained its central role as a jazz instrument or its modern jazz sonority. Styles of sax playing ranged from the slap-tongue technique of early Coleman Hawkins to the lyrical C-melody sound of Frankie Trumbauer. And so it was not necessarily opportunism and showmanship that led Paul Whiteman to attempt to push jazz into a new form, soon dubbed symphonic jazz or "symphonized syncopation." The "Experiment" at least held out the promise of being a daring exploration of an art form that, in the public's consciousness, was less than a decade old. Imagine what a concert purporting to survey the history of rock and roll would have sounded like in, say, 1956. Here was another apparently crude and wildly popular music with familiar and disreputable roots (boogie-woogie, race records, country music) and an unclear future. Could a prescient band leader have predicted the British invasion? Whiteman was, in his time, more recklessly prophetic than Leonard Bernstein, who was still explaining the origins of jazz to the classical audience in the mid-fifties and would not acknowledge rock until the post-Beatles late sixties.

Gershwin and Whiteman had collaborated before the *Rhapsody*. Whiteman recorded Gershwin's "South Sea Island" in 1921. The Whiteman Band played for the *Scandals of 1922*, a show that introduced "I'll Build a Stairway to Paradise." The show also included one performance of *Blue Monday* (which Whiteman would revive, to little avail, in 1925). In March 1923 Whiteman made a triumphant tour of England, where his band played for the revue *Brighter London*, and for small private parties given by Lord and Lady Mountbatten. On their return to America they were greeted with a well-orchestrated hero's welcome: Whiteman was crowned "King of Syncopation" at the Waldorf. Whiteman immediately began to plan a major concert for the band. The final impetus for the *Rhapsody*, however, came from a concert by the French Canadian singer Eva Gauthier at Aeolian Hall on 1 November 1923. She sang songs by Bartók, Hindemith, Milhaud and Schoenberg, but also by Irving Berlin, Jerome Kern, Walter Donaldson and Gershwin: "I'll Build a Stairway to Paradise," "Innocent Ingenue Baby" and "Swanee." Gershwin accompanied her in the American songs. Deems Taylor, writing in the *World*, reported that: "the singer reappeared, followed by a tall, black-haired young man who was far from possessing the icy aplomb of those to whom playing on the platform is an old story. He bore under his arm a small bundle of sheet music with lurid black and yellow covers. The audience began to show signs of relaxation; this promised to be amusing . . . Young Mr. Gershwin began to do mysterious and fascinating rhythmic and contrapuntal stunts with the accompaniment."[4] According to David Ewen: "At one point [Gershwin] made the audience purr with delight at the sly way in which he suddenly introduced a phrase from Rimsky-Korsakov's *Sheherezade* into the 'Stairway to Paradise'."[5]

Gauthier's recital inspired Whiteman to attempt something similar, but more ambitious. Goldberg suspects that: "Whiteman, who, after all, had received a symphonic training, felt more or less consciously a need for revindication. He wanted to justify jazz to the ways of the highbrows. In his own book [*Jazz*] for all his sentimental glorification of the commoners' taste in the arts, this feat of the solid musician, this desire to win the intellectual over, is clearly evident."[6] Soon afterwards he asked Gershwin to compose a piece for an all-jazz concert he would give in Aeolian Hall in February; Whiteman seized the date to beat his rival Vincent Lopez who had announced a similar jazz concert.[7] Legend has it that Gershwin forgot about the request until he read an article about the Whiteman concert in the *New York Herald Tribune* on 4th January which claimed that "George Gershwin is at work on a jazz concerto, Irving Berlin is writing a syncopated tone poem and Victor Herbert is working on an American suite." But, according to Thornton Hagert, his story about composing a theme on the train to Boston for the opening of *Sweet Little Devil* reveals that he was already composing in December.[8] The original manuscript, for two pianos, is dated 7 January 1924 – but Edward Jablonski, who gives the opening performance of *Sweet Little Devil* as 29 January, considers this to be the date on which

Gershwin began work. Grofé's rough score for the orchestration is dated 4 February 1924. Whether it was composed in ten days or three weeks – Gershwin's own accounts varied – the *Rhapsody* was not over rehearsed.

Whiteman announced his "Experiment" with a well-calculated series of promotional mixed signals. The pretentious hype for what was, after all, a dance band, might well portend a musical "emancipation" fitting for Lincoln's birthday, or it might all be a tongue-in-cheek excuse for some safe slumming. Highbrows and lowbrows lined up for tickets in the snow. David Ewen lists as present: Sousa, Damrosch, Godowsky, Heifetz, Kreisler, McCormack, Rakhmaninov, Stokowski, Rosenthal, Elman and Stravinsky, even though the last-named did not arrive in America until 6 January 1925.[9] Jablonski adds Mary Garden, Jeanne Gordon, Frances Alda, Amelita Galli-Curci and Alma Gluck, as well as Heywood Broun, Carl Van Vechten, Leonard Liebling, Gilbert Seldes and Henry O. Osgood (this group became Gershwin's supporters in the popular press) and also the novelist Fannie Hurst and Ernest Bloch, the only certifiably modernist composer in attendance.[10] In subsequent accounts the guest list expands and contracts like Soviet murals of the October Revolution.

Like other educators of American musical taste, Whiteman played many contradictory roles. He was a sophisticate and a lowlife, a Westerner who epitomized New York, a creator and exploiter, a classically trained violinist who functioned more as a manager and promoter than as a musician. He was called "King of Jazz" more, perhaps, for his royal appearance than his musical abilities – he looked like a playing-card king. And yet his orchestra demonstrated a kind of genius. Olin Downes captured Whiteman memorably: "He does not conduct. He trembles, wabbles, quivers – a piece of jazz jelly, conducting the orchestra with the back of the trouser of the right leg, and the face of a mandarin the while." On 12 February 1924, though, Whiteman took on the role of a professor. A pre-concert lecture assured (warned?) the audience that "the experiment is to be purely educational." If it succeeded it would "at least provide a stepping stone which will make it very simple for the masses to understand and therefore enjoy symphony and opera."[11] The lecture rolled out the old phrases of redemptive culture; it is not clear whether any of this was intended, or received, seriously.

Taken at face value, Whiteman's "Experiment" had a reasonable hypothesis: jazz had made tremendous strides over the decade since its beginnings, due to the "art of scoring." Thanks to Whiteman's arrangers, particularly Ferde Grofé, a raucous music improvised by illiterates had given way to the "melodious music of today, which – for no good reason – is still called jazz," played by trained musicians. The use of folk materials by European composers would have established a precedent for transforming the raw into the cooked, but it was not clear that this model of transformation would apply to jazz. Even some classical critics protested that much of Whiteman's artistry came at the expense of "hot" jazz qualities. Jazz arrangers of the future would seek to find a more idiomatic balance between composition and improvisation, discipline and swing – but that was yet to come.

We can judge the "Experiment" for ourselves thanks to two recent reconstructions.[12] Here is the complete program of the "Experiment in Modern Music" – with added critical asides:

Aeolian Hall
Tuesday Afternoon February 12, 1924 at 3 P.M.

PAUL WHITEMAN

AND HIS

Palais Royal Orchestra

ASSISTED BY

ZEZ CONFREY

AND

GEORGE GERSHWIN

PROGRAM

Part I

(1) True form of jazz

(a) Ten years ago – "Livery Stable Blues" La Rocca
(b) With modern embellishments – "Mama Loves Papa" Baer

The concert began by laying its hypothesis on the table – where it immediately went up in smoke. The paired numbers were supposed to contrast the old and the new, but the paradoxical effect, as Olin Downes put it, was to contrast the "Rabelaisian" with the "polite." Whiteman later expressed surprise when the audience did not take the performance of "Livery Stable Blues" as a parody: "I had the panicky feeling . . . that they were ignorantly applauding the thing on its merits." Like much else Whiteman said, however, this may have been a joke. "Livery Stable Blues" established the tone and subtext for the concert. It showed that respectable musicians could get down and dirty – and still remain respectable. The Original Dixieland Jazz Band recording of "Livery Stable Blues" was an enormous hit in 1917. It is a primitive novelty that advertises its own crudeness, a 12-bar blues repeated over and over without variations but with carefully planted barnyard breaks. It also displays the typical "gothic" texture of New Orleans jazz, with clarinet, trumpet and trombone pursuing independent lines against the additional overlay of barrelhouse piano and drums. The animal sounds are a kind of metaphor for the musical confusion – but also explain it away.

The absence of an obvious melody in "Livery Stable Blues" made it the perfect set-up for "Mama Loves Papa," a hit tune of the season. While we may be inclined to join Olin Downes in dismissing it as "polite," the arrangement (presumably by Grofé) demonstrated all the virtues of the Whiteman band: disciplined ensemble, a danceable beat, stylish harmonies and constantly changing textures. The trombone and trumpet solos, while hardly scorching, are respectable early examples of paraphrase improvisation. It may not swing, but one can hear the tune. "Mama Loves Papa" was the first of the many pop-tune fox-trots that filled the evening; it was to become increasingly clear that whatever the artistry of the arrangements, these numbers belonged more in the dance palace than the concert hall.

(2) Comedy selections

(a) Origin of "Yes, We have No Bananas" Silver
(b) Instrumental comedy – "So This is Venice" Thomas
(Featuring ROSS GORMAN)

Whiteman must have known that the audience would resist too much politeness (and there was plenty more to come), so he quickly turned to low comedy. "Yes, We have No Bananas" was both absurdly irrational and classical. Its tune is cobbled together from the Hallelujah Chorus and "I Dreamed I Dwelled in Marble Halls." "So This is Venice" allowed Gorman to display his abilities on clarinet, musette, trombone and saxophone. Through this stunt Whiteman was showing off the doubling skills that were essential to the stylistic range of the band. Note that both of these numbers, while burlesques, also tipped their hats to the audience's presumed knowledge of the classics.

(3) Contrast: legitimate scoring vs. jazzing

(a) Selection in true form – "Whispering" Schonberger
(b) Same selection with jazz treatment

In 1920, Grofé's arrangement of "Whispering" was Whiteman's first huge hit recording. It is an exemplary fox-trot. The melody is smooth and square, but the rhythm section gives it a double-time bounce. It is probably this ambiguous rhythmic effect – at once naughty and nice – that made the piece seem like a breakthrough at the time of its appearance. Whiteman never recorded a "true form" version of the song (I assume that the jazz treatment was his recorded version), so we cannot tell what contrast was offered.[13]

(4) Recent compositions with modern score

(a) "Limehouse Blues" Braham
(b) "I Love You" Archer
(c) "Raggedy Ann" Kern

Three popular show tunes in fancy Grofé arrangements. It is interesting to compare Whiteman's recording of "Limehouse Blues" with Fletcher Henderson's "Shanghai Shuffle" recordings from later in 1924. Despite the presence of Louis Armstrong, one modern critic writes: "The spongy saxophones and brittle trumpet trios have dated badly, and can be accepted only through the condescension of nostalgia."[14] That is a harsh way of saying how Whitemanesque the arrangement is, from the accented cross-rhythms to the oboe solo played by Don Redman. Whiteman's arrangement, by contrast, is anything but soggy, but it also never takes off the way the Henderson does with Armstrong's entrance. "Raggedy Ann," despite its brevity, is one of the most elaborate arrangements of the evening, and it demonstrates how Whiteman could offend purists of any school. It begins with a sweet, straight presentation of the tune for a trio of saxophones (*à la* Guy Lombardo), jumps to the minor for what Maurice Peress terms "a klezmorim chorus . . . worthy of Tevye"[15] then moves to a duo for musette (oboe with single-reed mouthpiece) and wa-wa trombone, only to end in a *William Tell* Overture gallop – all in three minutes. Whatever the aesthetic of the result, the amount and range of cultural information it contains is impressive.

(5) Zez Confrey (Piano)

(a) Medley of popular airs
(b) "Kitten on the Keys" Confrey
(c) "Ice Cream and Art"
(d) "Nickel in the Slot" Confrey
accompanied by the Orchestra

Zez Confrey, the guest star attraction of the program, pleased the crowd, though he was all but ignored by the critics, who concentrated on Gershwin. Perhaps Confrey lacked a publicity machine. But Confrey's fame, as well as his lack of aesthetic ambition, may have weighed against him. His "novelty" music was already familiar and he offered nothing novel either to thrill-seekers in the audience, or critics seeking a new American music. Confrey's solos also fit uncomfortably in an "orchestral" program. The music sprang from the piano and suffered in translation. Recordings by Confrey reveal that he was a superb pianist, the equal of Gershwin in flair and swing. But Confrey was also a one-trick pony – even though the trick was remarkable and had an enormous influence. Gershwin the pianist did not eclipse Confrey – but Gershwin the composer did so decisively.

(6) Flavoring a selection with borrowed themes

"Russian Rose"   Grofé
(Based on "The Volga Boatmen Song")

An elaborate confection by Grofé based on "The Volga Boatmen Song," Rakhmaninov's C-sharp minor Prelude, Rimsky-Korsakov's "Song of India" and Tchaikovsky's *1812 Overture* and *Marche Slave*. Thornton Hagert says that it "seems to characterize more than any other piece on the program, the pretensions to which Whiteman and Grofé so often succumbed throughout their association. It was the sort of thing which exasperated both serious critics and jazz fanciers to the point that they were often blinded to Whiteman's virtues." Peress wonders whether this was performed tongue in cheek; after all, Rakhmaninov was in the audience. The connections between Russian and American music, however, were strong at the time. Berlin, Gershwin and Copland descended from Russian-Jewish ancestry and their taste in classical music was Russo-French. Even the musically illiterate Berlin named Rimsky-Korsakov, Borodin and Musorgsky as his favorite composers.[16] The concert halls were dominated by Russian (and mostly Jewish) violinists and pianists, as the Gershwins burlesqued in their 1921 song "Mischa, Jascha, Toscha, Sascha." This created a natural bridge between the two worlds. Heifetz played Gershwin; Koussevitsky sponsored Copland.

(7) Semi-symphonic arrangement of popular melodies consisting of

"Alexander's Rag Time Band"   Berlin
"A Pretty Girl is Like a Melody"   Berlin
"Orange Blossoms in California"   Berlin

In 1924, Irving Berlin was the most famous composer of American popular song, and rumors had circulated for some time that he was about to embark on a symphonic or operatic project – endeavors for which he was in no way technically prepared. Whiteman apparently never asked Berlin's permission before he announced that the experiment would feature a new Berlin composition. Since none was forthcoming, Grofé arranged a suite of Berlin hits; the arrangements have not survived and were not recorded.

Part II

(1) Suite of Serenades Herbert

(a) Spanish	(c) Cuban
(b) Chinese	(d) Oriental

The fact that the audience, while eager for "hot" jazz, did not despise the classics was demonstrated in the ovation which greeted the *Suite of Serenades* of Victor Herbert, at the time America's most famous composer. Herbert represented the world of operetta. Though it is often said that the musical comedies of the twenties made operetta old-fashioned, the two genres co-existed well into the fifties. The stylish harmonies and orchestrations of Herbert's four miniatures demonstrate how the exoticism of operetta served as a means of absorbing up-to-date classical devices into popular music. Herbert's *Suite*, however, also shows why the audience was losing patience by the time Ross Gorman began his glissando and electrified the house. After "Livery Stable Blues", the program had drifted further and further from jazz.

(2) Adaptation of standard selections to dance rhythms

(a) "Pale Moon"	Logan
(b) "To a Wild Rose"	MacDowell
(c) "Chansonette"	Friml

Whiteman compounded the politeness of Herbert's *Suite* with three light classics played *à la* fox-trot. The novelty of this trick must have been wearing thin, and the "standard selections" themselves were rather faded, though Friml's *Chansonette* would return as "Donkey Serenade" in 1937.

(3) George Gershwin (Piano)

"A Rhapsody in Blue" Gershwin
Accompanied by the orchestra

Until Gershwin's appearance, Whiteman's concert offered a bewildering and gradually numbing miscellany of musical styles and genres. All the elements of a new music were there: jazz rhythms and colors, pop tunes, modern harmonies, virtuosic instrumental playing, lowdown fun and high-toned uplift. But only Gershwin produced a synthesis which placed these elements in a new relation. The concerto format of the *Rhapsody* itself introduced a dynamic element which had been missing. Gershwin created more than a piece of music, he created a dramatic persona. The audience did not just hear the product of musical cross-fertilization; in the interaction of the piano solo, played primarily in a romantic, rubato style which had appeared nowhere else in the program, with the carefully selected jazz antics of Whiteman's musicians, the audience witnessed the birth of a new cultural sensibility.

(4) In the field of classics

"Pomp and Circumstance" Elgar

Did anyone care?

Postscript

The Aeolian Hall "Experiment," instead of showing that melodious music had replaced "hot" jazz, demonstrated that one band could do it all: a large ensemble of skilled, literate musicians could play hot and sweet music with equal panache. It was also clear that the audience preferred its jazz "hot" rather than "melodious." In 1924, for white audiences at least, the *Rhapsody* passed for "hot." Whiteman repeated the program at Aeolian Hall on 7 March dropping "I Love You," "Raggedy Ann," "Nickel in the Slot," and "Pomp and Circumstance"; and at Carnegie Hall on 21 April, where the Berlin songs were jettisoned. When he took the concert on a national tour, beginning in May, Whiteman played down the condescending denigration of the "true forms of jazz." On the road the "Experiment" took on many of the trappings that look forward (at least conceptually) to today's stadium rock concerts, complete with light show. "The audience saw a curtain of gold cloth with a silhouette of the Whiteman orchestra; this withdrew to reveal the orchestra dressed in its summer whites and seated in white bentwood chairs on tiers of dove gray trimmed with vermilion. Two white grand pianos flanked the drummer's elaborate traps at the back of the stage, and behind them all was a glittering metallic curtain with huge vermilion floral designs. . . . To cap it all the stage was lighted (as it had been at Aeolian Hall) with shifting lights of green, yellow, pink, and blue."[17] The dramatic setting of the concert is well captured in the otherwise questionable biopic, *Rhapsody in Blue*. The glitzy decor of the concert, dismissed by some as circus-like, is yet another indication that Whiteman was operating in the mixed tradition of the American pops and appreciation concert, rather than the realms of serious music which was always more austere, or jazz which was often, as at the Cotton Club, far racier.

After the sold-out and ecstatically received tour the orchestra returned to New York in June where it recorded the *Rhapsody in Blue* and *Suite of Serenades* – and the Meditation from Massenet's *Thaïs*. The recording of the *Rhapsody* sold a million copies. According to David Ewen, "the royalties from the sale of sheet music, records, and other subsidiary rights gathered more than a quarter of a million dollars in a decade. The *Rhapsody* made Gershwin a rich man."[18] It did not hurt Whiteman either. The success of the *Rhapsody* altered his band's identity. The *Rhapsody* became its theme song. It was now as much a jazz band as a dance band, and Whiteman soon filled his orchestra with some of the finest jazz instrumentalists and singers in the country, including Bix Beiderbecke, Frankie Trumbauer, Bing Crosby and Mildred Bailey. He hired Don Redman and William Grant Still as arrangers. Yet he also expanded his string section (one of his cellists was the young William Schuman) and continued to give eclectic programs, including pop-tunes, comedy, novelty numbers and newly commissioned works by serious composers such as Roy Harris, David Diamond, Dana Suesse, Duke Ellington and Igor Stravinsky (*Scherzo à la Russe*). Whiteman and Grofé (whose *Grand Canyon Suite* nearly equaled the *Rhapsody* in popularity for decades) remained significant figures in American music, if not in jazz, through the fifties.

6

Interpretations

Gershwin's songs live on gloriously as performer's music; his concert works are prisoners of their scores.[1] Numerous attempts to revive the shows that gave birth to the songs have failed. But the songs do not need these period recreations. They have been reborn in the songbook albums of Ella Fitzgerald and Sarah Vaughan, or in Charlie Parker's *Embraceable You*. The *Rhapsody*, too, has been reinvigorated by the jazz performances of Glenn Miller, Duke Ellington and Marcus Roberts; but the inhibitions of "classical" music limit the possibilities of interpretation. These inhibitions have only increased as the *Rhapsody* has attained the stature of a concert classic, and with the rise of the notion of "authentic" performance. Today the printed scores, and particularly the "original" version, maintain an unchallenged tyranny. Performers feel obliged to invoke either the letter of the score or the spirit of the age to justify renditions which in fact do not vary all that much. Listeners often feel disappointed no matter what the technical polish or stylistic scholarship of the performers. Their uneasiness springs from the unclassical nature of the work itself. The musical style of the *Rhapsody* does not come out of the concert hall; it was imported into it from Broadway. Unlike contemporary concertos by Prokofiev, Ravel, Stravinsky or Bartók, none of which feels like period pieces (yet), the *Rhapsody* cannot be played as written. Performers either have to reconstruct an evanescent "authentic" style of performance, or have the courage to imagine a new one. Why should the *Rhapsody* be locked in a time capsule?

The performance history of *Rhapsody in Blue* spans three generations. During Gershwin's lifetime it was a piece of contemporary music closely associated with the performance styles of its original creators: Gershwin, Whiteman and Grofé. After Gershwin's death it soon acquired the status of a popular classic. This "pops" period overlaps with the

Second World War and the latter part of the standard-tune era when the sound of jazz shaped America's popular music. In the 1970s, the *Rhapsody* turned into a period piece, a remnant of the Jazz Age. Jazz itself seemed moribund; rock had taken its place as popular music. But at the same time the notion of authentic performance practice in early music led to a revival of the original version of the *Rhapsody*, free of all cuts. In less than seventy years the Rhapsody has evolved from an emblem of the future, to a relic of the past.

Although we can point to many outside forces to explain the changes in performance practice, the multifaceted nature of the *Rhapsody* itself has spurred these changes. Is it a jazz chart, a Broadway medley or a romantic concerto? It partakes of all three genres and an interpreter's choice of emphasis will affect the balance of elements. There are two polar conceptions of the score: as a classical text which needs to be played "as written" according to the "best" sources; or as a jazz text which serves as a framework for improvisation. The first approach descends from Gershwin's own recordings and piano rolls; the second from performances by Whiteman of his "theme song." And there are interpretations which mix elements from the two.

Gershwin's performances

Gershwin recorded the *Rhapsody* twice with Whiteman. An acoustic recording was made in June 1924 (Victor 55225); an electrostatic recording was made in April 1927, using Grofé's expanded orchestration of 1926 (Victor 35822).[2] Gershwin made a piano roll of the *Rhapsody* in two sessions. The extant recording of the Andante and finale dates from May 1925. The first half of the *Rhapsody* was issued in 1927. Kimball and Simon believe that both rolls date from 1925.[3] In 1993 these rolls were realized by Artis Wodehouse on the Yamaha Diskclavier.[4]

The recorded performances differ significantly from the piano rolls. They are cut, while the rolls are complete – indeed they are more than complete since they include both the piano and orchestra parts. At many points it seems obvious that passages have been overdubbed to include both parts. The piano-roll performance corresponds exactly to the two-piano four-hand score, except for the addition of Ross Gorman's ornamentation in bar 4 (which is printed in the piano solo edition) and a few details of rubato. This complete but monochromatic version of the *Rhapsody* sounds more unified than the versions with orchestra, even though Gershwin's performance differentiates between the solo and tutti passages. Two aspects of the piano roll conflict with later practice: the solo at rehearsal 25 is taken at a brisk tempo, and there are only a few, tantalizing, instances of swung eighth notes. In general, the rhythmic style of the performance is alternatively syncopated or rubato, but not swinging. The Love theme begins in four then accelerates; it is played in a consistently hyper-romantic style. Gershwin does not jazz the piece up.

The two recordings are far more polyvocal. By highlighting the most colorful jazz personalities in the Whiteman band – Gorman with his bent tones and slap-tonguing, Siegrist with his wa-wa trumpet and Maxon with his tail-gate, jazz-muted trombone – Grofé made the piece sound like a collaboration. The 1924 recording lasts just under nine minutes, due to major cuts in the scherzando and finale. This gives the impression of a piece with just two themes, both defined by the band in jazz style and then rendered classically by the piano. The E-major theme is played as a fox-trot, in strict tempo until six bars before rehearsal 31 when the counter-melody is allowed to dominate. The 1927 recording is the originator of what has become known as the "Hollywood Bowl" style of performance. Although it is slightly faster than the 1924 recording (and has identical cuts) it seems much more ponderous. The jazz licks sound like fading mementos; beginning with the clarinet glissando, they are performed portentously. The accompaniment barely sounds like a jazz band, but more like a Broadway pit orchestra. The one coherent remainder of the scherzo, the piano solo of the "Stride" theme, now sounds jazzier than anything else in the piece. The stylistic balance of the piece has shifted: the piano is now the jazz protagonist. The E-major theme begins fox-trot style and then is shmaltzed up to such a degree that Gershwin has to rush his own solo to make it fit on the recording.

The pops *Rhapsody*

After Gershwin's death his concert pieces became the most frequently performed works of any American composer. The version published in 1942 for symphony orchestra with vestigial saxophone and banjo parts served as the passport for the *Rhapsody*'s entry into the standard repertory. The *Rhapsody* and *Concerto in F* remained apart from the piano concerto literature in one important respect, however: they were never performed by the top pianists of the time, such as Rubinstein and Horowitz, but instead were taken up either by Gershwin specialists – like Levant and Pennario – or pianist/conductors – like Bernstein, Previn, Tilson Thomas and Levine. After the forties, Gershwin began to lose out to Copland and Barber in the classical repertory, and his music drifted to the pops concert, summer festival repertory. As time went on the performance style of the piece seemed to become increasingly problematic. We can observe this by comparing the popular recordings by Levant, Wild and Bernstein.

Oscar Levant was the most devoted of Gershwin's followers; he played the roles of parasite and court jester to Gershwin's genius – as his memoirs show. His recording with Ormandy and the Philadelphia Orchestra is a classic – or rather, is classicized.[5] It feels like a re-enactment. Levant's interpretation reproduces Gershwin's, and the wind players of the orchestra seem to have studied the Whiteman recordings closely. He respects the printed score except for one cut, which became canonical: the Trio. And yet the recording reveals a new aspect of the work. The Love theme ripens as it is played by the Philadelphia's famously rich strings, and a pretty tune turns into a major event in the listener's emotional history. The rhythm has also changed, with an exact doubling of the tempo at the third bar. The doubled speed only intensifies the romanticism of the counter-melody. The Russian heritage is now clear: the theme sounds more like Rakhmaninov than Lombardo. The *Rhapsody* as a whole had now shed almost all traces of jazz, except for a few details from the original recording preserved in wax.

Other pianists were less willing than Levant to adhere to Gershwin's style. Bernstein and Wild took the piece in two different directions. Earl Wild recorded the *Rhapsody* in 1960 with Arthur Fiedler and the Boston Pops.[6] It is the definitive pops performance of the period. The *Rhapsody* is played uncut in its 1942 garb. Wild performs the *Rhapsody* as if it were a classical concerto, and convinces the listener that it rewards virtuoso treatment through a wide variety of dynamics and touch. But what has happened to the band? The jazz solos now seem like token gestures; otherwise there is no jazz flavor at all, and the orchestra just serves to make noise between piano solos. The Andante is played like an anthem –

like a national anthem, which in some ways it had become. It is an exciting performance, but the piece seems to have lost some of its *raison d'être*.

Bernstein's 1959 recording with the New York Philharmonic Orchestra represents a crisis in the performance history of the piece.[7] (It should be studied along with Bernstein's contemporary essay on Gershwin as a manifestation of his "Gershwin problem.")[8] Despite an additional cut it is nearly four minutes longer than Levant's version. Nothing remains of the fox-trot, everything is dragged out ponderously to the point of (intended?) parody. The biggest departure from previous practice comes with the solo at rehearsal 25 which Bernstein plays as a slow and drunken blues – very much like his own blues "Big Stuff" from *On the Town*. The Andante becomes a funereal adagio. One feels that Bernstein was purposely inflating all the details of the *Rhapsody* in the hope that it would burst and disappear. By pushing the pretences of the piece beyond their musical limits Bernstein perhaps intended to demystify it. His performance, like his essays, demonstrates that the *Rhapsody* is not jazz, not modern music, not even a composition. But just as Bernstein said that no matter what you did to it, the *Rhapsody* remained the *Rhapsody*, Gershwin's piece survived Bernstein's assault.

The third generation of *Rhapsody* performances has been a conscious reaction against the pops style. Almost all recent recordings follow the original Whiteman arrangement without cuts, or even without the cuts that Gershwin made before the première. Richard Taruskin has argued that many "authentic" performances are really modern in character. Strict tempi and transparent textures are characteristics of twentieth-century neo-classicism which early-music performers have imposed retroactively on their own repertories. The same might be said about recent recordings of the *Rhapsody*. The idea seems to be to make it sound as much like *La création du monde* or *Threepenny Opera* as possible, by scraping away the romantic tinsel that has accrued to it since the 1927 recording. Re-creating the aura of the Whiteman band is quite a different matter.

Michael Tilson Thomas's two recordings typify the recent quest for authenticity. His 1975 recording[9] of the "original" featured a ghost appearance by Gershwin himself by using the 1925 piano roll – which had to be altered since it contained the band's parts as well as the solo. Yet the performance sounds neither like Whiteman's nor Gershwin's.

Tilson Thomas seems bent more on removing any trace of sentiment from the piece than on recapturing the feeling of the original performance. This is the *Rhapsody* with an attitude, lean and mean, some would say nasty, but unfortunately marred by awkward coordination with the mechanical soloist. It sounds like it was written in Mahagonny, not Manhattan. Tilson Thomas served his revisionist approach better when he recorded the solo part himself in the 1980s with the Los Angeles Philharmonic.[10] It's a warmer interpretation, reproducing many aspects of Gershwin's own recordings *con amore*. But its claims to authenticity are not entirely borne out. At rehearsal 25 Tilson Thomas surprisingly follows Bernstein's boozy blues rather than Gershwin's brisk rendition. And the Andante is in a modern style, the first two bars in a broad four, followed by a doubled tempo. It seems hard for any performers, no matter how historically informed, to give up the full-blown romantic approach to the theme in favor of a more authentic rendition that usually sounds saccharine.

Perhaps the most successful "authentic" recording to date is the version conducted by Maurice Peress with Ivan Davis on piano.[11] This recording reinstates some of the material Gershwin cut before the première, but these turn out to be minor variants. The particular strength of this recording is the superb performance by Davis. His performance has the rhythmic finesse of the first recording without slavishly imitating Gershwin's every gesture. Peress also rediscovers how to play the E-major theme as a two-beat fox-trot without losing the romantic patina the theme has acquired over the years.

Jazz performances

Rhapsody in Blue has enjoyed a second performance history as a jazz piece. This line of descent has been less inhibited by the printed page. It was Whiteman's theme song, and his style of playing it depended on the setting: straighter for dancing; soupier for concerts. The popular successor to Whiteman's version was Glenn Miller's 1941 recording with Bobby Hackett on trumpet.[12] It would be possible to reconstruct much of the evolution of jazz from the early 1920s through the Swing Era by studying the fine details of Miller's recording. The instrumental colors and harmonic voicings transpose the *Rhapsody* from Whiteman's sound-world to the equally idiosyncratic one of the Miller Orchestra, which was in many ways the cultural heir to Whiteman. Bill Finegan's arrangement turns the piece into a rhapsody for trumpet and big band – at least for the first half which reinterprets the opening of the *Rhapsody* before jumping to the Andante tune. Finegan enhances the romantic aspects of the piece with a slow but slightly swung tempo while at the same time brings it up to date in terms of jazz style.

By contrast, Duke Ellington's 1960 arrangement of the *Rhapsody* is a brilliant act of deconstruction – and renewal.[13] Starting with Harry Carney's refusal to glissando in the opening, no detail is left unchanged. Through such outrageous impiety Ellington rediscovers the jazz essence of the piece; his is the only version that swings. Ellington also rediscovers the genius of Grofé's original scoring. He builds his arrangement on solos by Carney, Cootie Williams, Ellington, Paul Gonsalves, Johnny Hodges and Jimmy Hamilton. By placing the clarinet last instead of first Ellington shows how thoroughly he has turned the piece upside down. He thereby returns the *Rhapsody* to the jazz instruments from which it sprang. If I could own only one version of *Rhapsody in Blue* this would be it.

Marcus Roberts's recent recording of the *Rhapsody* is the polar extreme from "authenticity."[14] Roberts rescored the piece for orchestra *and* jazz ensemble, changed many of the harmonies of the piano solos, and extended the length of the piece to nearly half an hour. Rather than trying to recapture a historical moment, Roberts builds his performance on the historical irony that Gershwin's *Rhapsody* predates most of jazz history. What would Gershwin have done had he heard Louis Armstrong, Earl Hines or Errol Garner? Roberts's recomposition of the *Rhapsody* provides something of an answer to that question – though perhaps an overly literal one, full of recognizable allusions to the jazz that stands between today and 1924. Roberts also confronts Gershwin with the phenomenon of jazz improvisation. He opens up the score by inserting a long series of improvised choruses, only loosely related to the changes of Gershwin's tunes. He thereby juxtaposes two modes of performance – re-creation and creation – and also two modes of listening – the cumulative mode with which we follow a composed piece from beginning to end, and the cyclical mode we use in listening to a series of improvised choruses. The clash between composition and improvisation raises issues that apply as much to the music of Duke Ellington, Thelonious Monk and Charles Mingus as they do to Gershwin. As often happens when musicians are allowed to blow choruses on a Mingus tune, the Gershwinesque sources of the music soon turn into generic jazz that could be played in any setting. It is fascinating, however, to think about how much less linear our expectations of musical listening are today than just a few years ago when the charge of "formlessness" was an aesthetic indictment. The form of Roberts's maxi-*Rhapsody* is much looser than Gershwin's, yet it successfully creates an environment for the work which questions it and honors it at the same time.

7

Influence

Rhapsody in Blue was a hard act to follow, even for Gershwin. Its only successful progeny were Gershwin's *Concerto in F* and Ravel's Piano Concerto in G; more problematic offspring – if we limit the field to works that would not have been written without the example of the *Rhapsody* – are James P. Johnson's *Yamekraw* and Gershwin's two later piano and orchestra works, the *Second Rhapsody* and the *"I Got Rhythm" Variations*. The twenties produced many jazz symphonies both before and after the *Rhapsody*, most of them independent of Gershwin's example. Satie's *Parade*, Stravinsky's *L'histoire du soldat*, Hindemith's *Suite 1922* and Milhaud's *La création du monde* all preceded the *Rhapsody*. Honegger's Concertino (which Rosenfeld praised at the expense of Gershwin's *Concerto*)[1] and Krenek's *Jonny spielt auf* are continuations of Euro-jazz. Kurt Weill's version of symphonic jazz would only show the strong influence of Gershwin after he emigrated to the United States. In America a number of jazz symphonies made an initial impact almost equal to the *Rhapsody*'s: John Alden Carpenter's *Krazy Kat* (1921) and *Skyscrapers* (1926); Louis Gruenberg's *Daniel Jazz* (1925), *Jazzettes* (1926) and *The Emperor Jones* (1933); George Antheil's *Jazz Symphony* (1925) and *Transatlantic* (1930). Jazz also permeated works written in the 1920s by Virgil Thomson (*Sonata da chiesa*), Sessions (Symphony no. 1) and Copland (*Music for the Theater*, Concerto for Piano and Orchestra). The hostile reception accorded Copland's "jazz" Concerto indicates how far he and most of the other jazz symphonists were from Gershwin. Critics saw these pieces as extensions of European modernism despite their jazz flavoring; none sprang from the milieu of popular music.

Among Gershwin's contemporaries the only American composers who pursued a course similar to his were James P. Johnson and William

Grant Still, both of whom were active in the musical theater. Johnson's concert works have had a frustrating history; none was published in complete form and few are recorded. Still's symphonic works are only now receiving their due.[2] While both composers had some contact with Gershwin, it is problematic to speak of influence, especially since Johnson's piano style and his "Charleston" had such an important impact on Gershwin. Still's symphonies and the concert works of Florence Price and William Levi Dawson probably would have been written without Gershwin's example; the works of the latter two composers owe far more to the example of Dvořák's "New World" Symphony. But in their frank use of popular melodies and populist romantic style Johnson's *Jazz-a-mine Concerto* and Still's *Afro-American Symphony* share an aesthetic position with Gershwin which distinguishes them from most other American composers of the period.

Concerto in F

> Lady Jazz, adorned with her intriguing rhythms, has danced her way around the world. . . . But for all her travels, and her sweeping popularity, she has encountered no knight who could lift her to a level that would enable her to be received as a respectable member in musical circles . . . George Gershwin . . . is the prince who has taken Cinderella by the hand and openly proclaimed her a princess to the astonished world, no doubt to the fury of her envious sisters.[3]

Less than a year after the "Experiment," Gershwin crossed over from symphonic jazz to jazz symphony with his three-movement piano concerto, commissioned by Walter Damrosch for the New York Symphony Orchestra. Although it never matched the fame of the *Rhapsody*, critics at the première and ever since have viewed it as a leap forward – a *Petrushka* to the *Rhapsody*'s *Firebird*. Gershwin wrote the *Concerto in F* for a standard symphony orchestra with no jazz instruments. He proudly claimed the orchestration as his own, although it is clear that he received advice from experienced orchestrators: Will Vodery, Robert Russell Bennett and in particular, Bill Daly (who later denied playing anything more than an advisory role).[4] Aside from the difference in forces, the *Concerto* displays a wealth of formal invention and warmth of emotion that were barely hinted at in the *Rhapsody*. And yet the *Concerto* shares many elements, and flaws, with the *Rhapsody*. Like the *Rhapsody*, the *Concerto* probably grew from pre-existing materials; some of these were published in 1926 as the three Preludes.[5] The *Concerto* uses blues themes, a Confreyesque train theme, two E-major love themes and a percussive toccata figure as well as a recurring main theme that equals the Slavic *Weltschmerz* of any tune by Rakhmaninov. Most of the themes imply a pop-tune structure, but with their cadences systematically lopped off. There are also undistinguished linking passages and novelty-piano-style cadenzas. Yet the *Concerto* seems both more warmly romantic and more jazzy than the *Rhapsody*.

The rhythms of the Charleston and Black Bottom dominate the first movement. Both dances had been around for some time. Noble Sissle claimed that he learned the Charleston in Savannah in 1905.[6] James P. Johnson, who wrote the hit song "Charleston" for the black musical *Runnin' Wild* (1923), said that it was a cotillion step as early as 1913. The Black Bottom dates from at least as early as 1907, when Perry Bradford wrote his Jacksonville Rounders' Dance, which he turned into the Original Black Bottom dance in 1919.[7] The two dances were related and often confused. The second strain of Jelly Roll Morton's "Black Bottom Stomp" (recorded in 1926) is in Charleston rhythm. The Black Bottom rhythm, though, plays a secondary role in the first movement of the *Concerto*; the Charleston rhythm and large fragments of Johnson's melody play as central a role in the *Concerto* as the "Man I Love" tag did in the *Rhapsody*.

The principal idea of the second movement is a blues which owes more to the "race" blues of Bessie Smith than to Handy. The delicate scoring for clarinet trio and muted trumpet sounds like a transcription of the recordings Smith made with Fletcher Henderson or James P. Johnson on piano.[8] Although the first statement of the blues theme is sixteen bars long, its structure follows the classic 12-bar design (which Gershwin had not used in the *Rhapsody*). The extra four bars in the first statement of the theme are just an echo.

The "modernism" of the *Rhapsody* also returns in the *Concerto*, but in an updated form – as the percussive opening immediately proclaims. The powerful tune that the piano plays at its first entrance is written on the tones of an A flat blues scale, though Gershwin approaches the blues third through the downward leap of a major seventh – something he would never do in a show tune. He also harmonizes the first four bars of the melody with parallel major sevenths between the melody and the bass. The first four bars are harmonically ambiguous, hinting at both major/minor and diminished-seventh qualities; only in the next four bars is the tonal direction made clear. In the second statement of the tune (rehearsal 5) Gershwin adds a descant in the violas which, at least for the first phrase, gives the appearance of bitonality (see Ex 7.1). The second movement begins with another token of "modernism" – parallel triads – but the most modernistic writing in the movement comes at its carefully prepared climax (rehearsal 16) where the level of dissonance suggests early Schoenberg more than Debussy. The third movement, which Gershwin called an "orgy of rhythm," updates the Confreyesque cross-rhythms of the *Rhapsody* with hints of Stravinsky. There are also parallel thirteenths that recall Ravel (two bars before rehearsal 12). But these stylish effects do not seem tacked on; they are a logical extension of Gershwin's own idiom.

Ex. 7.1 *Concerto in F*: main theme

Ravel's Piano Concerto in G

On 8 March 1928 Maurice Ravel wrote to Nadia Boulanger:

> There is a musician here endowed with the most brilliant, most enchanting, and perhaps the most profound talent: George Gershwin.
>
> His world-wide success no longer satisfies him, for he is aiming higher. He knows that he lacks the technical means to achieve his goal. In teaching him those means, one might ruin his talent.

> Would you have the courage, which I wouldn't dare have, to undertake this awesome responsibility?[9]

Boulanger declined, perhaps picking up subtle hints from Ravel about the problems involved in teaching someone who had already achieved such success. Ravel had already turned Gershwin down himself after being dazzled by him at a dinner party the night before he wrote to Boulanger. According to Eva Gauthier, Ravel had told Gershwin that if he studied with him he "might lose that great melodic spontaneity and write bad Ravel."[10]

I like to imagine that Ravel did give Gershwin a composition lesson, but it took the form of the G Major Concerto.[11] Although jazz is not its only stylistic source, Ravel's Concerto remains the greatest compliment ever paid by a European composer to American music. Ravel tips his hat to the *Rhapsody* in his own E-major theme (and anticipates Cole Porter's "Blow, Gabriel, Blow" with another). The third movement is a cross between the Toccata of Ravel's *Tombeau de Couperin* and the "rhythmic orgy" of Gershwin's *Concerto in F*. But, having shown these signs of respect, Ravel provides Gershwin with a lesson about economy of means in form and orchestration – it is a lesson Ravel could have taught many other composers. Ravel's Concerto is entirely devoid of the weak links that glue Gershwin's movements together. It is written as one continuously unfolding melodic line that moves back and forth with elegance and precision from orchestra to piano. Even the cadenza of the first movement does not interrupt the melodic line, but is part of a strict recapitulation.

Ravel's orchestration also exposes the flabbiness of Gershwin's scoring. Ravel usually assigns the melody to a single instrument. The first movement of his concerto is a succession of solos: piccolo, trumpet, E-flat clarinet, trombone, bassoon. Each instrument is used in a distinctive range: the piccolo is placed low so that it sounds like a tin whistle; the bassoon plays in its highest register so that it sounds like a crooning tenor. With the exception of the opening and close of the slow movement of the *Concerto in F*, Gershwin is rarely so precise in his effects. He doubles lines, perhaps more out of a concern for volume than color. For the big tune at rehearsal 20 of the first movement, for example, Gershwin has the English horn play along with all of the violins (on their G string). The English horn player must feel badly used. Although much of Gershwin feels overscored (Virgil Thomson cattily called it "gefilte fish orchestration"),[12] the sonority is consistent with his full-textured song-plugger style of piano playing. Early in his life Gershwin had learned the advantages of making a big noise.

James P. Johnson: *Yamekraw* (Negro Rhapsody)

Yamekraw is a fascinating African-American parallel to *Rhapsody in Blue*. Like the *Rhapsody* it was written for a jazz concert. The première took place at Carnegie Hall on 27 April 1928 at a concert produced by W. C. Handy and the poet Robert Clairmont. All the music was by African-Americans: Handy, Joplin, J. Rosamond Johnson, James A. Bland and James P. Johnson. The composer, acknowledged as the greatest practitioner of stride piano, was not present, however. He was conducting performances of his musical *Keep Shufflin'* (orchestrated by Will Vodery) and, oddly enough, could not get out of that obligation for the première. Fortunately Fats Waller filled in, to great effect. Variety wrote: "Waller's torrid interpolations at the ivories stopped everything."[13] The concert was more of a success for Waller than for Johnson.

Like *Rhapsody in Blue*, *Yamekraw* was written (and published) for piano and then orchestrated by another hand, in this case by William Grant Still.[14] It was also assembled from pre-existing materials: Johnson borrowed Spencer Williams's "Sam Jones Done Snagged His Britches" as well as his own "Georgia's Always on My Mind."[15] The Williams tune, however, was itself clearly indebted to the spiritual "Every Time I Feel the Spirit."

Despite these similarities, *Yamekraw* makes a very different impression from Gershwin's *Rhapsody*. Its themes – a spiritual, a blues and a characteristically black-music theater song – all come from African-American traditions. Despite a few classically tinged transitions, the piano style of the work derives from stride, or from the style developed by Harry Burleigh for accompanying spirituals. Perry Bradford, who published the piece as a piano solo, described it as a "genuine Negro treatise on spiritual, syncopated and blues melodies expressing the religious fervor and happy moods of the natives of Yamekraw, a Negro settlement on the outskirts of Savannah, Georgia."[16] Whatever the ethnographic basis of the work, its religious fervor is obvious; this was an emotional terrain

Gershwin would not approach until *Porgy and Bess*. The form of *Yamekraw* similarly relies on African-American traditions rather than invoking classical models. As in Johnson's stride-piano compositions, the piece unfolds as a series of varied choruses, always respecting the phrase structure of the original melodies or, in the second movement, the blues.

Yamekraw is an act of ethnic definition, a pulling together of elements from the African-American musical tradition, not a bridge between those traditions and European music. Although the leaders of the Harlem Renaissance tended to resist jazz ("upper crust Afro-Americans still mostly recoiled in disgust from music as vulgarly explosive as the outlaw speakeasies and cathouses that spawned it"),[17] Johnson's composition epitomized the program of that short-lived literary movement. As Samuel Floyd Jr. has written of *Yamekraw*: "This was Renaissance style – exactly in keeping with the dreams and goals of Renaissance leadership and masses."[18]

Ellington: *Creole Rhapsody*

Gershwin's success may have delayed Duke Ellington's critical recognition, much as it stood in the way of Copland's. Both composers only achieved widespread critical recognition after Gershwin's death. Gershwin had claimed center stage of American music; once he was gone Copland moved in the direction of greater popularity, and Ellington was finally able to write a major extended work for Carnegie Hall: *Black, Brown and Beige*. Ellington may have been perplexed by Gershwin, though he rarely revealed his feelings. After a leftist interviewer provoked Ellington into disparaging *Porgy and Bess*, Ellington claimed he had been misquoted and worked hard to smooth things out.[19] Ellington stated, in the interview, that if he were to write an opera it would be "true to and of the life of the people it depicted. The same cannot be said for *Porgy and Bess*."

Although Ellington may well have felt that he could express the experiences of his people more authentically than Gershwin, the musical styles and artistic ambitions of the two composers have much in common. Both combined blues melodies with rich chromatic harmonies; both extended song forms into larger instrumental compositions. In some songs Ellington seems to be consciously following in Gershwin's footsteps. "Black Beauty" opens with the same harmonic progression as the Ritornello theme of the *Rhapsody*; "In a Sentimental Mood" begins exactly like "Someone to Watch Over Me." In both cases, though, Ellington immediately puts his own stamp on the music. His melodies, usually conceived for instruments rather than voice, are both freer in shape and bluesier than Gershwin's. "Someone to Watch Over Me" seems overly rigid in its many internal repetitions, while "In a Sentimental Mood" flutters up and down without any exact repeats. Most of Ellington's extended compositions owe little to Gershwin.[20] *A Tone Parallel to Harlem* might be termed an African-American parallel to *An American in Paris*, but Ellington's idiom and forms are his own. *Creole Rhapsody*, however, sounds like a deliberate response to *Rhapsody in Blue*, though it may have begun as a publicity stunt. According to James Lincoln Collier, Ellington's manager Irving Mills told the Chicago press that Ellington would give the première of an extended Rhapsody – the next day. Ellington purportedly stayed up all night to compose the piece. But, according to Collier, the piece had already been recorded; Mills was trying to make the headlines.[21] Nevertheless, the story of a rhapsody being written in short order by a jazz composer had a familiar ring to it. A clarinet glissando soon after the opening of the piece makes the connection between the two rhapsodies clear.

Ellington recorded *Creole Rhapsody* twice: on 20 January 1931 for Brunswick, and on 11 June for Victor. The two versions are virtually different pieces. The earlier version is six minutes long, is played in a single tempo and has three themes: an opening "modernistic" eight-bar motto, a blues and an irregularly phrased trombone duet. The second version is eight minutes long and in changing tempos. It replaces the trombone theme with a lyrical pop-tune reminiscent of "In My Solitude," played by Arthur Whetsol (trumpet), interrupted briefly by a killer-driller up-tempo chorus by Johnny Hodges (alto saxophone). While the second version eliminates most of Ellington's piano solos, it resembles *Rhapsody in Blue* more than the first. Towards the end this connection is made explicit, as A. J. Bishop noted: "This final section borrows elements from the link between the middle and final parts of Gershwin's *Rhapsody in Blue*, and has a feeling of heavy-handed pretentiousness which was absent from the first recording, and this, together with its jerky stop and go character, does a lot to spoil the Victor record."[22] Schuller concurs with this judgment: "despite (or more likely, because of) some subtle 'borrowing' from Gershwin's *Rhapsody in Blue*, the last minute or so does not hang together too well."[23] Aside from a couple of minor-third sequences (which stem from the eight-bar motto) the most overt reference to Gershwin in this section is a big augmented-fifth dominant chord similar to the one before the *agitato* section at the end of the *Rhapsody*. Otherwise Ellington's episodic conclusion is more of a parallel to Gershwin's than an imitation of it. In the first version of *Creole Rhapsody* Ellington had ended simply and effectively by bringing back the eight-bar motto and fading it out over a snare-drum ostinato. For the second version Ellington, like Gershwin, attempted to sew together more of the elements of the piece towards its close; the new lyrical tune, like the *Rhapsody*'s Love theme, had changed the emotional climate of the piece and could not just be dropped. Ellington drew additional expressivity from the tune by presenting it as an out-of-tempo duet for clarinet (Barney Bigard in his haunting low register) and piano. This moment of self-reflection is the most rhapsodic in *Creole Rhapsody*, and owes nothing to Gershwin.

Second Rhapsody and *"I Got Rhythm' Variations*

In a publicity picture taken of Gershwin and Koussevitsky before the première of the *Second Rhapsody* in 1932 both men wear pained expressions. Neither man was the other's choice of a collaborator. Koussevitsky was Copland's patron, and Gershwin had first tried to have Toscanini conduct the première. The piece had not been commissioned, but emerged from music Gershwin had written for the movie *Delicious*. It began, according to Ewen, as a "six-minute orchestral sequence describing the sounds and movements of the city and highlighted by the rhythm of riveting."[24] Only one minute was used in the movie; the *Second Rhapsody* was, appropriately for the time, a salvage operation. The last monuments of the boom – the Empire State Building, George Washington Bridge and Rockefeller Center – were being finished as the Depression set in; the actual rhythms of riveting would soon be silenced, replaced by the cries of Apple Marys. The *Second*

Rhapsody has suffered since its première from the feeling that Gershwin was no longer the spokesman for the age. The *New Yorker* opined that the work offered "nothing but rhythms now grown trite."[25] Despite recent claims that it is the sleeping beauty of Gershwin's oeuvre it remains rarely performed and, at this late date, not even published in an orchestral score. Gershwin's publisher suppressed his orchestration in favor of an "improved" version by Robert McBride commissioned by Frank Campbell-Watson.[26]

The *Second Rhapsody* shows signs of Gershwin's growing musical sophistication – not always an improvement. The entire work grows from the "rivet" rhythm. Unfortunately this figure consists of eight eighth notes, and it imposes a squareness on all the themes that no amount of cleverness can hide. Gershwin was in effect tying both hands behind his back by trying to construct a piece almost entirely out of unsyncopated themes using equal note values (see Ex. 7.2). Most damagingly, the squarest part of the piece comes first. The rivet theme appears as a rumba that never takes flight – "just another rumba" to quote the title of a much better Gershwin tune. An even-note but off-the-beat lyric theme which Gershwin called "Brahmsian" offers a welcome

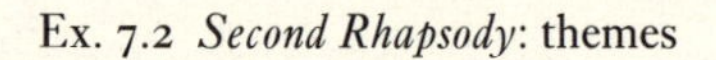
Ex. 7.2 *Second Rhapsody*: themes

respite, but the rumba just keeps going. Gershwin shows a surer touch in the second half of the piece, which begins at rehearsal 21 with a bluesy A-major love theme over a rising chromatic bass line (as in "Liza"). He cross cuts the love theme (which anticipates Arlen's "Stormy Weather") cinematically with a chorale, developing both elements with growing intensity – but then those rivets return.

Whatever its failing, the *Second Rhapsody* illustrates Gershwin's ever-expanding harmonic vocabulary. Although most of his "modernist" techniques still derive from Debussy, Gershwin saturates the music with passing dissonances and harmonic clashes (see, for instance, seven bars before rehearsal 19) that give it a distinctive undertone of angst. The *"I Got Rhythm" Variations*, written while Gershwin studied with Schillinger, take the pursuit of dissonant harmony to a new constructivist level.[27] The piece begins with an interval expansion and contraction of the four-note "I Got Rhythm" motif, from seconds to thirds, to fourths to sevenths – and back again. Later it builds four-note chords by "verticalizing" the motif. An eight-note chromatic counter-subject follows a contracting wedge shape that implies an all-interval pattern. A "Chinese" variation abounds in parallel fourths and minor seconds. It's all very clever, and a little relentlessly overblown (like much of Gershwin's music of the early thirties). Fortunately, Gershwin's lyrical side comes to the fore in the 'Valse triste' variation, and even more in the breezy blues that alternates with a simple chorale whose pandiatonic harmonization points to the subsequent directions of Gershwin's music far more powerfully than the Schillingeresque exercises that surround it (see Ex. 7.3).

Ex. 7.3 *"I Got Rhythm" Variations*: pandiatonic harmonization

8

Invisibility: ideology and reception

In the history books

At the time of its première many listeners (though not all the music critics) saw *Rhapsody in Blue* as an embodiment of both jazz and musical modernism, a novel and titillating emblem of the Jazz Age. Modern music was a hot subject in Manhattan that winter. Besides Varèse's *Octandre*, which followed close on the première of his *Hyperprism*, the previous months had seen the New York premières of Schoenberg's *Herzgewächse* and Stravinsky's *Le sacre du printemps.* It was natural for some critics to hear Gershwin's *Rhapsody* as an American retort. Henry Osgood, a Gershwin supporter, claimed that Stravinsky's *Le sacre* and Honegger's *Pacific 231* "had nothing to say and said it cleverly, but Gershwin spoke with intelligence and conviction."[1] The conservative Daniel Gregory Mason, by contrast, dismissed *Le sacre* and the *Rhapsody* together as "tweedledum and tweedledee."[2] But as Carol Oja has documented,[3] the modernist composers grouped around Aaron Copland (who had arrived back in New York from Paris six months after the première of the *Rhapsody*) soon drew the line between themselves and Gershwin. Paul Rosenfeld, the most progressive music critic on the scene, articulated their view in unflattering comparisons drawn between Copland and Gershwin. Rosenfeld brusquely dismissed Gershwin as a

> gifted composer of the lower, unpretentious order; yet there is some question whether his vision permits him an association with the artists. He seems to have little feeling for reality. His compositions drowse one in a pink world of received ideas and sentiments. *Rhapsody in Blue* is circus-music, pre-eminent in the sphere of tinsel and fustian.[4]

The modernists – Copland, Thomson, Sessions – did not reject the use of jazz, but they modeled their jazz works on the examples of Stravinsky,

Milhaud and Satie. Copland, whose Russian-Jewish background was similar to Gershwin's, later claimed that they inhabited separate spheres of operation:

> In many ways Gershwin and I had much in common – both from Brooklyn, we had studied with Rubin Goldmark during the same time and were pianists and composers of music that incorporated indigenous American sounds. But even after Damrosch commissioned Gershwin's *Concerto in F* for performance in the same season as Koussevitsky premièred my *Music for the Theatre*, Gershwin and I had no contact. We must have been aware of each other, but until the Hollywood years in the thirties, moved in different circles. On one occasion when we were finally face to face at some party, with the opportunity for conversation, we found nothing to say to each other![5]

When Copland surveyed "America's Young Men of Promise" for *Modern Music* in 1926 he made no mention of Gershwin. Years later he explained the omission: "George Gershwin . . . was famous in 1926 but down in everyone's book as a composer of popular music with only two concert pieces to his credit."[6] Copland was clearing a path for himself. He also swept Henry Cowell aside as "an inventor, not a composer."

The subsequent fate of the *Rhapsody* in the critical accounts of jazz and modernism says more about the evolving ideologies of music history than about Gershwin's music. The term "modern" music narrowed from a blanket term for any new music that did not sound old-fashioned, to a more prescriptive meaning. After World War I the modernist school and its attendant infrastructure of journals, concert series and festivals separated and protected new music from both the established concert world and the market place. The central position attained by the Schoenberg school after the Second World War confirmed this critical evolution. Modern music and popular music seemed to speak in unrelated languages.

The term "jazz," first applied around 1916 to a rough and sexy strain of African-American music, soon became synonymous with any syncopated mass-marketed popular music. All this changed after the Second World War when jazz suddenly stopped being popular. With the decline of swing and the rise of bebop, rhythm and blues, and rock 'n' roll, jazz was gradually redefined as a kind of art music with its own canon of masterpieces. Jazz criticism began to use the language of modernism and shared its preoccupations with technical breakthroughs and vangardist posturing: "radical" became synonymous with "good," and Frankfurt School contempt for the popular became a recurring motive.[7]

Although some of the earliest books on jazz, such as Osgood's *So This is Jazz* and Whiteman's *Jazz*, place Gershwin at the center of their stories, he barely figures in more recent jazz history books. The early writers were proponents of symphonic jazz, a short-lived phenomenon that influenced big-band swing and film music but not mainstream jazz improvisation. Much jazz history through the fifties, especially that found in high school and college texts, emphasized the most popular musicians of the Swing Era: Goodman, the Dorseys, Glenn Miller, Woody Herman – all of whom were white. The corrective rewriting of jazz history in the past four decades has fortified the African-American foundations of the jazz canon: Morton, Oliver, Bechet, Armstrong, Redman, Ellington, Basie – and so on. But Gershwin, who never claimed to be a jazz musician, is not so easily omitted from jazz history. The harmonic structure of "I Got Rhythm" is second only to the blues as the basis for jazz improvisation[8] and Gershwin's songs remain an inexhaustible quarry for jazz performers.[9]

Gershwin's treatment by jazz historians exposes many sensitive issues, especially since much jazz criticism has turned on the questions of "what is and what is not jazz." Because critics have defined jazz as a performer's art whose essence lies in improvisation, they have, until recently, given little attention to *any* composers. Critics deemed jazz composition secondary to improvisation, and often reviewed symphonic compositions by jazz composers with hostility. Even the most distinguished accomplishment of jazz composition, the oeuvre of Duke Ellington, has been considered exceptional.

Many recent jazz histories, compensating for the imbalances of the past, present jazz not just as an essentially African-American music, but as an exclusively African-American music, and push major white jazz figures beyond the peripheries of the genre. Eileen Southern's encyclopedic *Music of Black Americans*, hardly a polemical text, nevertheless presents the *Rhapsody* as a slick appropriation:

> It was an ironic twist of fate that the world should receive its first symphonic work written in the jazz and blues style not from William

> Grant Still, who was firmly grounded in the musical lore of his people, but from the white composer George Gershwin, who had only superficial contacts with Negro music in his visits to Harlem and to the all-black shows on Broadway.[10]

Music history is full of similar ironies: the most famous "Spanish" opera is by a Frenchman, the most famous "Hungarian" dances by a German and the most famous "Egyptian," "Japanese" and "Chinese" operas are by Italians. Southern is correct in pointing out how easy it was for white musicians, European and American, to appropriate a musical style they barely knew. Gershwin certainly was not grounded in the roots of jazz as were Still, Johnson or Ellington – but he had an empathy with African-American music that amounted to an identification. Wilfred Mellers is perhaps the only critic to have understood how *Porgy and Bess* could "spring so deeply from Gershwin's own experience."[11]

The parallel evolutions in the understanding of the categories "modern music" and "jazz" left *Rhapsody in Blue* in a critical limbo which, however, has not diminished its popular appeal. The issue of form, a recurrent motive of *Rhapsody* criticism, often masked a fear of popularity. *Rhapsody* earned a huge amount of money because it was copyrighted both as a composition and as a song.[12] Commercial music and art music, particularly of the modernist kind, followed divergent economic paths. To borrow a useful distinction from Richard Crawford: modernist music is essentially composers' music, while songs are performers' music.[13] In the music of, say, Stravinsky or Bartók, form, content, harmony and instrumentation are fused in ways which make rearrangement or cutting difficult. Stravinsky notoriously denied any interpretive role to performers; the composer claimed full artistic control of the music. By contrast, copyright law defines a song not as its arrangement or form, but as its melody. This allows performers a wide degree of latitude in interpreting and arranging a song, while also greatly expanding the number of performances, from the concert hall to the juke box, from which a composer could extract the payment of royalties. Although popular classical music of the past, like the arias of Verdi, also became performers' music, the new legal understanding that led to the creation of ASCAP and other licensing agencies allowed the composer to benefit handsomely from broad and varied usage. The *Rhapsody* may be the only piece of twentieth-century concert music to have earned its composer a fortune – but much of this was due to the sale of sheet music and recordings of shortened versions. Gershwin made substantial cuts in both the 1924 and 1927 recordings of the *Rhapsody* so it could fit on 78 rpm disks. While we might assume that Gershwin resented the need to make cuts – and he did "record" the complete *Rhapsody* on a piano roll – the recordings in effect sanctioned the cuts. For many listeners who grew up listening to them, the short form of the *Rhapsody* was the *Urtext* – and the complete form sounded bloated and redundant.[14]

Ideological contexts

The reception history of *Rhapsody in Blue* demonstrates the impotence of music criticism. Rather than weeping along with Lawrence Gilman over the "lifelessness of its melody and harmony, so derivative, so stale, so inexpressive,"[15] audiences immediately embraced the *Rhapsody* and the concert world soon found an abiding place for it. The first reviewers sounded all the salient themes: the originality and flair of some or all of the materials, the questionable relation to jazz, the looseness of form. The sourest responses came from other composers, whether conservative like Daniel Gregory Mason or modernist like Virgil Thomson. The journal *Modern Music* kept up a stream of anti-Gershwin articles in the thirties. This did nothing to diminish the popular appeal of the music and by the forties Thomson was comparing Gershwin to Schubert.[16]

The musical criticism of the *Rhapsody*, however, reflects broader ideological debates about the nature of the arts in modern society. During the twenties the *Rhapsody* loomed large in discussions of the Jazz Age. Since the thirties its critical reputation has reflected the evolving understanding of the mass media and culture industry. Both of these ideological frames, however, treat the *Rhapsody* as a cultural object; as an emblem, its own voice was muted. In looking at the cultural controversies surrounding the *Rhapsody*, I am less interested in deciding which side of an argument was right than in identifying the common ways in which the symbolic connotations of the *Rhapsody* were identified and manipulated. Most of these strategies had little to do with Gershwin's aesthetic goals, or the popular understanding of his works.

The Jazz Age debate

> That we owe the change to Prohibition is certainly arguable. By putting all social intercourse in America on an alcoholic basis, it forced people to dance when they were not quite themselves . . . the simple beat of the tom-toms was the safest of all, so it came in.[17]

> Soon after this primitive step became established ballroom dancing began to show the disturbance that shook all of polite society when the lid of segregation was taken off of vice and the bordello erupted into the drawing room.[18]

> The word jazz in its progress towards respectability has meant first sex, then dancing, then music.
>
> It was characteristic of the Jazz Age that it had no interest in politics at all.[19]

Jazz arrived in New York along with the Red Scare and the beginning of prohibition, as well as women's suffrage. The euphoria of victory soon gave way to the fear of immigration and Bolshevik revolution. The arrival in the northern cities of large groups of blacks from the south led to the first race riots in Chicago in July 1919. The Ku Klux Klan gained a wide following, its ideology popularized by D.W. Griffiths' *Birth of a Nation*. Young people reacted to these tensions by overthrowing their parents' puritanical values in favor of a long-repressed hedonism, well suited to a rapidly expanding economy. As Ann Douglas notes, "immense gains with no visible price tag seemed to be the American destiny."[20] F. Scott Fitzgerald caught the apolitically rebellious temper of the time in *This Side of Paradise*, and the Jazz Age was born – almost before there was jazz.

The link between jazz and subversion, intoxication and criminality – and blacks and Jews – colored its reception throughout the twenties and beyond. Jazz was seen either as a cover for anti-social, barbarous activities or, as Ann Douglas has shown, as the emblem for a lifestyle revolution based on a self-conscious "frankness" that was taking the place of an older idealism.[21] In fact, the line between idealism, honesty and criminality was hard to draw; prohibition turned the majority of Americans into criminals. Breaking one taboo allowed one to break others involving sex and drugs, and Harlem after dark became the preferred site for such activities among white sophisticates – music was not necessarily the main draw. Gershwin was a familiar figure in Harlem. Gershwin's supporters like Gilbert Seldes (author of *The Seven Lively Arts*), Carl Van Vechten (author of *Nigger Heaven*) and drama critic Alexander Woolcott were leading figures of the new urbanity.

The aesthetic of the Jazz Age repudiated an older tradition of redemptive culture. For older composers like Charles Ives and Daniel Gregory Mason, as Macdonald Smith Moore has shown,[22] the spiritual core of art transcended the materialism of American society. For Mason, though certainly not for Ives, spiritual values were also racial:

> This Anglo-Saxon element in our heterogeneous national character, however quantitatively in the minority nowadays, is qualitatively of crucial significance in determining what we call the American temper. . . . In our literature the type is immortally enshrined in the work of Emerson and Thoreau.[23]

The threatening elements in American culture were also racial:

> Our whole contemporary aesthetic attitude toward instrumental music, especially in New York, is dominated by Jewish tastes and standards, with their Oriental extravagance, their sensuous brilliancy and intellectual facility and superficiality, their general tendency to exaggeration and disproportion.[24]

In completely different ways Ives and Mason attempted to keep alive an American Eden, whether located in the rural New England of Ives's boyhood or in the pure forms of non-commercial chamber music cultivated by Mason.

Gershwin's supporters celebrated a new post-Edenic America: an urban, diverse society developing its own forms of expression. Replacing one road to redemption with another Seldes put himself forward as the Luther of a cultural reformation:

> If there were an Academy I should nail upon its doors the following beliefs:
>
> That Al Jolson is more interesting to the intelligent mind than John Barrymore and Fanny Brice than Ethel;
>
> That Ring Lardner and Mr. Dooley in their best work are more entertaining than James B. Cabell and Joseph Hergesheimer in their best;
>
> That the daily comic strip of George Herriman (Krazy Kat) is easily the most amusing and fantastic and satisfactory work of art produced in America today;

> That Florenz Ziegfeld is a better producer than David Belasco;
>
> That one film by Mack Sennett or Charlie Chaplin is worth the entire oeuvre of Cecil B. Demille;
>
> That Alexander's Ragtime Band and I Love a Piano are musically and emotionally sounder pieces of work than Indian Love Lyrics and The Rosary;
>
> That the circus can be and often is more artistic than the Metropolitan Opera House in New York;
>
> That Irene Castle is worth all the pseudo-classic dancing ever seen on the American stage; and
>
> That the civic masque is not perceptibly superior to the Elks' Club Parade in Atlantic City.[25]

Seldes was a discerning critic of the young Gershwin: "His sense of rhythm, of an oddly placed emphasis and color, is impeccable."[26] He had doubts, however, about Gershwin's evolution. In 1934 he wrote that Gershwin's music was becoming "more complicated and interesting and brittle and unmelodious with every year."[27]

In praising the new mass art forms, Seldes promoted a kind of cultural realism; Van Vechten sounded more like a lifestyle revolutionary. As early as 1917 he predicted the coming of a jazz-based American music;[28] and he urged Gershwin on to greater things after the *Rhapsody*:

> Go straight on and you will knock all Europe silly. Go a little farther in the next one and invent a new *form*. I think something might be done in the way of combining jazz and the moving picture technique. Think of the themes as close-ups, flashbacks, etc.![29]

In his bohemian life and aesthetic tastes Van Vechten seems to have been Daniel Gregory Mason's worst fears come true – all the worse because, like Paul Whiteman and Cole Porter, he was not "oriental." But Van Vechten celebrated what Mason demonized. The defining themes of the Jazz Age were primitivism and mechanization. Both Whiteman and Gershwin compared their music – favorably – to machinery:

> Jazz . . . evolves new forms, new colors, new technical methods, just as America constantly throws aside old machines for newer and more efficient ones.[30]

Whether you loved them or loathed them, the Primitive and the Urban-Modern were both easily made visible as the black and the Jew – or some fusion of the two. Nearly every review of Gershwin in the twenties noted his swarthy appearance, which was often photographed amidst the art deco furnishings and modern paintings of his Riverside Drive apartment. He was a musical Valentino, ready to sweep away the virginal figure of American culture.

If dark sensuality was one emblem of the Jazz Age, the Jewish criminal or parvenu was another. To some critics the important role played by Jews in the new cultural forms was a source of hope. In a review of the *Rhapsody* that appeared in *The Nation*, Henrietta Straus wrote:

> one cannot but wonder whether this now Slavic, now Oriental element in jazz is not due to the fact that many of those who write, orchestrate, and play it are of Russian-Jewish extraction; whether, in fact, jazz, with its elements of the Russian, the Negro, and the native American, is not that first distinctive musical phase of the melting-pot for which we have been waiting so long and which seems to have such endless possibilities.[31]

Straus's philo-Semitic stance, however, cannot quite be taken at face value. For the German-Jewish establishment the melting pot was a way of cleansing the Eastern European Jews of their offensive qualities. But it is notable that she would hear the *Rhapsody* as a "refined" product of the melt-down process.

For other writers the Jew was a less benign figure. He appears as the hairy-nostrilled Meyer Wolfsheim, fixer of the 1919 World series, in *The Great Gatsby*, and as the arrogant Robert Cohen in *The Sun Also Rises*. But in musical terms there was no need to imagine similar characters. Berlin, Gershwin and Copland were three variants of the type – and were described by admirers and detractors in terms of the stereotype. Cutting Gershwin down to size, Virgil Thomson in 1935 sounded all the overtones:

> His invention is abundant, his melodic quality high, although it is inextricably involved with an oversophisticated commercial background. That background is commonly known as Tin Pan Alley. By oversophisticated I mean that the harmonic and orchestral ingenuity of Tin Pan Alley, its knowledge of the arts and presentation, is developed out of all proportion to what is justified by the expressive possibilities of its musical material. That material is straight from the melting pot. At best it is a piquant but highly unsavory stirring-up-together of Israel, Africa,

> and the Gaelic Isles. In Gershwin's music the predominance of charm in presentation over expressive substance makes the result always a sort of *vers de société*; and his lack of understanding of all the major problems of form, of continuity, and of straightforward musical expression, is not surprising in view of the impurity of his musical sources and his frank acceptance of them.[32]

In Thomson's presentation, Gershwin's eclecticism becomes a form of miscegenation. Thomson's style is so witty that some may dismiss these excesses as a joke; Mason, however, put things more squarely: "The Jew and the Yankee stand in human temperament, at polar points; where one thrives, the other is bound to languish." But it was left for an English musician, Constant Lambert, to expose the full anti-Semitic subtext:

> The fact that at least ninety per cent of jazz tunes are written by Jews undoubtedly goes far to account for the curious sagging quality – so typical of Jewish art – the almost masochistic melancholy of the average fox-trot. This masochistic element is becoming more and more a part of general consciousness, but it has its stronghold in the Jewish temperament. . . . There is an obvious link between the exiled and persecuted Jews and the exiled and persecuted Negroes, which the Jews, with their admirable capacity for drinking the beer of those who have knocked down the skittles, have not been slow to turn to their advantage. But although the Jews have stolen the Negroes' thunder, although Al Jolson's nauseating blubbering masquerades as a savage lamenting, although Tin Pan Alley has become a commercialized Wailing Wall, the only jazz music of technical importance is the small section of it that is genuinely Negroid. The "hot" Negro records still have a genuine and not merely galvanic energy, while the blues have a certain austerity that places them far above the sweet nothings of George Gershwin.[33]

The Jewish middleman was seen as the enemy of the black primitive; Jewish eclecticism as the opposite of authentic, anthropological modernism. Moore sums up the perceived threat of cultural disorder well:

> Most troublesome for friends of Yankee classicism, Jews tried to participate in the sacred ceremonies of national autogenesis through culture. It seemed that Jewish composers intended to obliterate the root distinction between high culture and merely anthropological culture. Classical and vernacular, traditional and avant-garde, white and black, hedonism and mechanism: all appeared to enter the Jewish melting pot.[34]

In their fear of cultural leveling, modernists joined hands with reactionaries of both New England and the Bible Belt in rejecting Jewish influence. Gershwin, the dark handsome product of the lower East Side, Mr. Nobody from nowhere (as Tom Buchanan calls Gatsby) suddenly taking the music world by storm, would serve as one symbol of the cultural subversion of the Jazz Age, alongside the jungle goddesses, Bessie Smith and Josephine Baker.

Masscult, midcult and the culture industry

Jazz Age New York stood for modernity; in retrospect it seems charmingly pre-modern. The mass media were in a formative stage: the movies were silent, radio was in its infancy, recording technology still crude. Cultural life revolved around live performance, whether in the theater or the concert hall. And to some extent culture remained "bourgeois" rather than modern. Jürgen Habermas defines bourgeois culture as a balance of roles:

> Bourgeois art had two expectations at once from its audiences. On the one hand, the layman who enjoyed art should educate himself to become an expert. On the other hand, he should behave as a competent consumer who uses art and relates aesthetic experiences to his own life problems.[35]

The literary and concert worlds of New York remained largely bourgeois in this sense. They aimed at popular success from an informed audience, at least informed by the daily press. As Ann Douglas points out, Fitzgerald, Hemingway and even Faulkner wrote best-sellers. Many artists of the period, like Gershwin, were "high lowbrows eager to capture mass acceptance and elite adulation in a single stroke." Douglas sounds an ominous note of things to come, however, when she claims that: "The 1920s were the first and perhaps the last moment when something like the practice of free will was possible in the consumer society and entertainment culture America was fast becoming."[36] By the end of the twenties most of the infrastructure of modern mass media was in place, and the Frankfurt School would define the new culture industry in terms of a totalitarian determinism.

Where Gilbert Seldes saw the new mass art forms as lively, T. W. Adorno saw them as vehicles of repression. His arguments about pop music often seem confused because of his loose use of the term "jazz," but it is clear that he has Gershwin's music, with its Slav melancholy and gliding harmonies, very much in mind:

> The function, for instance, of the standardized Slav melancholy in the musical consumption of the masses is incomparably greater than that of the greatest moments in Mozart or the young Beethoven. The leverage of music – what they call its liberating aspect – is the opportunity to feel something, anything at all. But the content of the feeling is always privation. Music has come to resemble the mother who says, "Come and have a good cry, my dear." In a sense it is a kind of psychoanalysis for the masses, but one which makes them, if anything, ever more dependent than before.[37]

> It [popular music] makes do, throughout, with the depraved stock of late Romanticism: even Gershwin is a talented transposition of Tchaikovsky and Rachmaninoff into the amusement sphere.[38]

For Adorno, the malignant culture industry controlled the lives of the helpless masses through illusory amusement. His ideas influenced American thinking from the late thirties on, but they were modified, and depoliticized, significantly. Former Trotskyite intellectuals used Frankfurt School language when they abandoned populist art in favor of high modernism. Clement Greenberg defined modernism narrowly in terms of specialization; each art pursued its particular nature to discover its pure form. Anything mixed was suspect; and so the enemy became not all of popular culture, but "kitsch":

> To fill the demand of a new market, a new commodity was devised: ersatz culture, kitsch, destined for those who, insensible to the values of genuine culture, are hungry nevertheless for the diversion that only culture of some kind can provide.[39]

By the fifties the imported term "kitsch" had been translated as "midcult," but was still demonized in Frankfurt School terms:

> So let the masses have their Masscult, let the few who care about good writing, painting, music, architecture, philosophy, etc., have their High Culture, and don't fuzz up the distinction with Midcult.[40]

> Middlebrow culture . . . insinuates itself everywhere, devaluating the precious, infecting the healthy, corrupting the honest, and stultifying the wise.[41]

Even though they smoothed out Adorno's knottier arguments, the cultural critics of the fifties, as Andrew Ross has noted, "largely agreed with the picture which the Frankfurt School provided of a populace of dopes, dupes and robots mechanically delivered into passivity and conformity by the monolithic channels of the mass media and the culture industries."[42] They accepted a bread and circuses model of popular culture, though they often made allowances for "authentic" forms of popular expression in jazz or folk music, or even the occasional movie. But the vast mid-section of American culture – Broadway musicals, Hollywood movies, television sitcoms, variety shows, the Book of the Month Club, and the nascent rock and roll – was seen as a threat to true art, mass produced in order to drug the public. Gershwin's music was premised on a mediation between cultural spheres. Frankfurt School cultural criticism closes off the discussion because it believes that any "negotiation" is an illusion. In its critical theory the Jazz Age figures of the melting-pot middleman and the black primitive hardened into the social configurations of the culture industry and the regressive mob. The "amusement" sphere, no matter what its charms, is always a version of the Roman Coliseum. Its products and its audience are robbed of any role as subject, of any authentic voice. In American cultural polemics, however, Adorno's global despair fractured into a partisan dispute between "high" neo-conservatives and "low" cultural diversifiers. The cultural center seemed to evaporate, and Gershwin's treatment by music historians dwindled to the passing, condescending nod.

The making of Americans: Yiddish culture, Jewish Blackface, an American Rhapsody

Gershwin was neither a primitive nor a Svengali. His music has outlived the Jazz Age, and even the pop-tune era. The critical discourses surrounding it, whether they were used positively or negatively, seem to be at odds with the musical content. Can we retrieve its ideological voice? To do so we must turn to the actual cultural milieu in which Gershwin grew up, the Lower East Side of New York, and trace Gershwin's passage through the melting pot.

It is hard today to imagine the powers of self-creation exercised by the first American-born children of Eastern European Jews. The process that transformed Izzy Baline, who arrived from Russia at the age of five and grew up in extreme poverty, into Irving Berlin would be hard to reproduce today; yet it was emblematic of a whole generation, and served Gershwin as a prototype for his own journey. Representations of assimilation range from the sentimentalized melodrama of *The Jazz Singer* to the tragic realism of Abraham Cahan's novel *The Rise of David Levinsky*, a favorite of Ira Gershwin's. The first generation faced a frightening range of possibilities. Some, broken by the hardships of tenements and sweatshops, clung to the past and cursed the so-called "golden land." Others broke all connections with the past and assimilated as quickly as possible. Few paths out, legal or not, were barred; compared to Europe, America placed few restrictions on Jewish ambition. In New York the Educational Alliance and City College were stepping stones to culture and the professions, but the developing entertainment business and crime were equally plausible escape routes from the squalor of the slums. Entertainment, music, theater and, soon, the cinema allowed the transformational experience to achieve formal expression, though often in disguise.

The cultural milieu of the Lower East Side centered on the Yiddish theater which staged its first production in 1882 and flourished for the next sixty years. According to Charles Schwartz, Gershwin started frequenting the Yiddish theater around 1913, and was particularly interested in the music theater works of Joseph Rumshinsky and Abraham Goldfaden.[43] At the time that Gershwin was just starting out as a song plugger, the Yiddish theater may have offered comparative security, and Gershwin might well have considered a career as a Yiddish composer. Apparently his talents gained rapid recognition. In 1915, Boris Thomashevsky, the greatest star of the Yiddish theater (and grandfather of Michael Tilson Thomas), invited Gershwin to collaborate on a Yiddish operetta with Sholom Secunda, a well-known composer of Yiddish songs best remembered for "Bei Mir Bist Du Sheyn." Secunda, a conservatory graduate, rejected the idea of working with an untrained youngster, and Gershwin never returned to the Yiddish theater. He retained close ties to its cultural world, however; in 1929 he was commissioned by the Metropolitan Opera to write a work based on the classic Yiddish play *The Dybbuk*. That opera was never written, but it could be argued that *Porgy and Bess*, with its transplanted shtetl setting and celebration of "little people," stems as much or more from Yiddish theater as from any African-American source.

The Yiddish theater was a popular venue which mixed high and low elements in order to engage, move and elevate its audience. Irving Howe claims that "there was no such theater anywhere else in the world, a theater of the unwashed plebes rather than the decorous bourgeoisie."[44] He notes how central the mixed character was: "It is characteristic of the Yiddish theater . . . that together with *shund* [trash] it should also turn to productions of Shakespeare, Schiller and Goethe [and, later, Ibsen, Hauptmann, Shaw, Wilde and Maeterlinck] done in hopeless translations but also reflecting an innocent respect for culture."[45] *Shund* plays were melodramas that aimed shamelessly at the emotions of the audience; they survived the best efforts of intellectuals at raising all of Yiddish theater to a higher level, because they were closest to the lives, and hearts, of the audience. The audience was part of the experience: "[they] relished the details, often demanded that songs be repeated . . . shouted denunciations of villains and showed no displeasure with the mixture of tragedy and vaudeville, pageant and farce – nor even the intrusion of personal affairs in the midst of performances."[46] It was an emotional theater; Thomashevsky would always sing a song about Mama and the audience "found it impossible to hold back their tears."[47] Howe notes that "the audiences cared more about expressiveness than coherence, more about moments of vision than organized themes."[48] At the same time, though, the Yiddish theater was open to dramatic innovation coming from Europe; the founding of the Yiddish Art Theater, with the production of *Farvorfen Vinkel* in 1918,[49] began a phase of serious experimentation that would leave its impact on all American theater, especially through the ideas of the Actors Studio, created by graduates of the Yiddish theater.

The relation between *shund* and serious theater was an ongoing controversy of Yiddish theater – its unresolvable central dialectic. Its eclecticism was ideological and ethical. As a theater of the people it collapsed distinctions between high and low. As Howe says, "eclecticism – as the aesthetic corollary of multilingualism, eternal wandering and *galut* [exile] – was in the very nature of the Yiddish theater."[50] The subject of Yiddish theater was nothing less than the Jewish people, not the Jewish religion. It presented a view of humanity symbolized by the figure of *dos kleyne menshele* (the little man), poor, anti-heroic, "anti-Promethean" as Howe says – yet enduring. Gershwin would give *dos kleyne menshele* musical expression in the figure of Porgy. Ironically, the high art form of opera lent itself better to the ethos of Yiddish theater than did the "sophisticated" venue of the Broadway musical.

Irving Howe's loving reconstruction of the milieu of Yiddish theater sidesteps a crucial point. Yiddish theater remained, despite its socialist politics and occasional experimentation, a link with the past; it served as a vehicle of expression for the losers, those immigrants who were not able to drop their old identities and assimilate. Even if Sholom Secunda had agreed to work with Gershwin on a Yiddish operetta, the project could not have thwarted Gershwin's ambitions to be an American and create American music. For many Jewish entertainers of the period, the road to America passed through the mask of blackface. During the period from 1910 to 1929, Jewish entertainers dominated and transformed this century-old American theatrical style. Al Jolson, Eddie Cantor, George Burns and George Jessel performed in blackface, as did Sophie Tucker, the last of the red-hot mamas. Gershwin's "Swanee" became his first hit as a vehicle for Al Jolson, in blackface.

The institution of blackface is painful to discuss; it created and sustained powerful stereotypes that controlled the interaction between whites and blacks in America. As Houston Baker says:

> By misappropriating elements from everyday black use, from the vernacular – the commonplace and commonly sensible in Afro-American life – and fashioning them into a comic array, a mask of *selective* memory, white America fashioned a *device* that only "counts" in relationship to the Afro-American system of sense from which it is appropriated. The intensity of the minstrel ritual, its frantic replayment to packed and jovial houses, is a function of the "real" Afro-Americans just beyond the theater's doors, beyond the guttering lights of the mind's eye. The device is designed to remind white consciousness that black men and women are mis-speakers bereft of humanity – carefree devils strumming and humming all day – unless, in a gaslight misidentification, they are violent devils fit for lynching, a final exorcism that will leave whites alone.[51]

By 1910, blackface was just one version of stereotyped theater, including broad Jewish stereotypes, in which Jews performed. Yet blackface was perhaps the crucial rite of identity transformation. As Howe writes:

> the blackface persona, bringing a freedom of the anonymous and forbidden, could become so powerful a force that sometimes the entertainer felt a need to make it clear that it was only a persona. After one of her stomping exhibitions in blackface, Sophie Tucker would peel off a glove and wave to the crowd "to show I was a white girl." A surprised gasp would rise from the audience, then a howl of laughter, as if in tribute to all that impersonation could dredge up.[52]

Jewish performers did not merely wear a mask, they seemed to fuse into it. Isaac Goldberg wrote: "Put Yiddish and black together and they spell Al Jolson."[53] Jewish performers brought to blackface the sentimentality of the Yiddish theater; they transformed the old comic form into a schmaltzy, lachrymose, but sexy vehicle.

There are different ways of answering the question posed by Michael Rogin: "Why should the member of one pariah group hide his identity under the mask of another?"[54] As the pariahs of Europe, Jews could easily identify with the sufferings of the African-American; but they soon learned that American society would treat them far better than it would blacks. Yet while blacks might be lower in the social order than Jews, they were also, by being Christian, at once more American and more religious than the immigrant Jews, many of whom had abandoned any religious practice. African-Americans were also more embedded in American history, however tragically, than Jews would ever be. Jewish blackface was thus a complex phase of cultural negotiation which partook of identification and indifference, idealization and condescension, admiration and envy. Howe interprets Jewish blackface as "one woe speaking through the voice of another."[55] Ronald Sanders describes it as cultural pastiche, "a gift of peoples who live in culturally ambivalent situations . . . as Jews have throughout their long history."[56] Rogin questions the element of identification: "Switching identities, the jazz singer acquires an exchange value at the expense of blacks. . . . Stereotypes located within both pariah groups were exteriorized as black, embraced as regenerative, and left (along with actual blacks) behind."[57] In Gershwin's case, at least, Rogin's analysis is misleading. Gershwin's career began with "Swanee," a blackface song, and ended with *Porgy and Bess*, a folk opera which was explicitly written for performance by a black cast; Gershwin rejected the idea that Porgy be played by Jolson in blackface.[58]

Jewish blackface sustained older stereotypes, but the mask allowed Jewish performers to give emotions which they had abandoned in the ghetto an American form. Thomashevsky's mama songs became Jolson's "Mammy." The embarrassing old-world wailing of the orthodox *schul* turned into the religious fervor of "Gone, Gone, Gone." Even the chant of the bar mitzvah ritual turned into "It Ain't Necessarily So." Assimilating to white America meant the cultivation of pep, drive and efficiency; blackface allowed repressed sentimentality and religion to surface anew. For many Jewish entertainers, however, the passage of blackface not only left the actual blacks behind, as Rogin says, but Jews as well. The movie *The Jazz Singer* was virtually the last representation of clearly identified Jews on screen until the 1950s.[59] The Jewish stereotypes of *The Jazz Singer*, maudlin mama-worship and the medieval disorder of the synagogue, died along with blackface. While black actors would now personify blacks on screen, albeit in stereotyped roles, Jews only appeared furtively. Jewish audiences "knew" that Paul Muni, John Garfield and Sylvia Sidney were representing Jewish characters no matter what roles they actually played, much as gay audiences learned to decode the masks of closeted actors.

Gershwin's short career took him across a minefield of cultural issues, yet he seemed to retain an innocent nobility. In 1965, in his review of Wilfred Mellers's *Music in a New Found Land*, Virgil Thomson stated the conundrum in a surprisingly sugared form:

> Gershwin came from Tin Pan Alley, by the way of the Lisztian rhapsody, to giving a Broadway play operatic status. And although the theme of that is a white man's view of Negro life (hence phony throughout), its translation into melody is a lovely one because Gershwin was a pure heart.[60]

Gershwin's biographies, such as they are, do not support Thomson's billet-doux. They portray him as selfish, narcissistic, emotionally stunted, occasionally cruel. Yet the music remains as "pure" as Thomson claims. In a sense, Gershwin's whole project was present in 1918 when he and Ira wrote "The Real American Folk Song (Is a Rag)." Like the Yiddish theater, his music served as an emotional connection between a plebeian audience and a dream of high culture; its ideal was always folk music. Paradoxically, though, the "real" folk music would be a manufactured pastiche, an artifice fusing Jewish and African-American elements into a form that would claim to be uniquely American. The modern folk song, folk opera or folk rhapsody would not be an exercise in nostalgia, but a way of understanding the modern world. The historian Warren Susman identified Gershwin's distinctive gift to his audience:

> in Gershwin's hands the folk material is used not to justify a refusal to accept the new order of things but to help us to understand what we must ultimately come to grips with, while his use of collective dreams and hopes, basic instincts, and illusions provides a sense of identity for those who find themselves aliens in an alien world.[61]

Notes

1 Introduction: The one and only

1 25 November 1987.

2 That threat and the fact that the *Rhapsody* was already public domain in many countries probably kept the licensing fee at a relatively modest level.

3 "Why Don't You Run Upstairs and Write a Nice Gershwin Tune?" in *The Joy of Music*.

2 Identity

1 Bernstein, *The Joy of Music*, 52–53.

2 For the development of copyright law as related to music see Sanjek and Sanjek, *American Popular Music Business in the 20th Century*, and Ennis, *The Seventh Stream: the Emergence of Rocknroll in American Popular Music*.

3 *The Washington Post*, 25 November 1987.

4 Schwartz, *Gershwin: his Life and Music*, 295.

5 Armitage, ed., *George Gershwin*, 28.

6 See Hagert, liner notes for *An Experiment in Modern Music. Sweet Little Devil* opened in New York on 21 January 1924.

7 Goldberg and Garson, *George Gershwin: a Study in American Music*, 138.

8 *Gershwin*, 66.

9 *Gershwin: His Life and Music*, 78. In a footnote Schwartz cites Vernon Duke's claim (made in 1947) that "Gershwin could ill conceal his grudging admiration for the roly-poly Grofé, who was just as much at home among brasses and woodwinds as Gershwin was in the company of his beloved piano" (p. 295).

10 See Shirley, "Scoring the Concerto in F," and "The Trial Orchestration of Gershwin's Concerto in F."

11 Armitage, ed., *George Gershwin*, 30–31.

3 Instruction manual (instead of an analysis)

1 George Gershwin in Armitage, ed., *George Gershwin*, 188.
2 Ira Gershwin in ibid., 20.
3 Jablonski, *Gershwin*, 65.
4 Rosenberg, *Fascinating Rhythm*, 56.
5 *The Music of Gershwin*, 56–71.
6 "It was not until rehearsals of the *Rhapsody* began that the glissando accidentally came into being. According to Grofé, who of course was present at rehearsals, the opening clarinet passage at first was played "straight" as written by Ross Gorman, Whiteman's virtuoso solo clarinet and an incredible performer on other wind instruments as well. Then, stated Grofé, as a joke on Gershwin and to enliven the often-fatiguing rehearsals, Gorman played the opening measure with a noticeable glissando, stretching the notes out and adding what he considered a jazzy, humorous touch to the passage. Reacting favorably to Gorman's whimsy, Gershwin asked him to perform the opening measure that way at the forthcoming concert and to add as much of a 'wail' as possible to the upper notes of the clarinet run. Gorman even experimented before the concert with various reeds until he found the one that gave him the most 'wailing' sound . . ." Schwartz, *Gershwin: his Life and Music*, 81–83.
7 This structure is clearer in the original version of the theme, heard on the Peress recording, which restates A before moving on.
8 Armitage, ed., *George Gerswhin*, 122.
9 Thomas, *A Virgil Thomson Reader*, 24; *Modern Music* 13/1 (November 1935), 13–19.
10 George Gershwin in Hyman Sandow, "George Gershwin to write a New Rhapsody," *Musical America*, 18 (February 1928), 5.

4 Ingredients

1 Zora Neale Hurston quoted in Ogren, *The Jazz Revolution*, 134.
2 Badger, *A Life in Ragtime,* 194.
3 J. W. Henderson, "Current Opinion," *New York Herald Tribune* (September 1924).
4 *Virgil Thomson Reader*, 15.
5 "Jazz Structure and Influence," *Modern Music*, 4/2 (Jan./Feb. 1927), 9–14.
6 Ewen, *A Journey to Greatness*, 41. See Tucker, *Ellington: the Early Years*, 87–91 for more information about Baron Wilkins.
7 Charters and Kunstadt, *Jazz: a History of the New York Scene*, 31.
8 Badger, *A Life in Ragtime*, 94.

9 *Ibid.*, 116.
10 Stearns and Stearns, *Jazz Dance*, 97.
11 *Ibid.*
12 *Stride: the Music of Fats Waller*, 9–10.
13 He purchased an eight-volume leather-bound edition of Debussy's piano music when he visited Paris in 1928.
14 See Charles Hamm's *Yesterdays* for a detailed discussion.
15 Kimball and Simon, *The Gershwins*, xxiv.
16 *The Memory of All That*, 114.
17 Davis, *The History of the Blues*, 69.
18 *Ibid.*, 68–69.
19 Wilder, *American Popular Song*, 3–28.
20 Mark Tucker (letter to author) cautions that this division is deceptive; some of the popular blues singers, like Mamie Smith, were performing popular songs in a vaudeville style.
21 Hamm, *Yesterdays*, 487.
22 *The History of the Blues*, 6.
23 Jimmie Lunceford recorded a hot Sy Oliver arrangement of this song as "Swingin' Uptown" in 1934.
24 "The Jijibo" of 1923 attempts to repeat this winning formula.
25 *American Popular Song*, 127.
26 An excerpt from *Blue Monday* is possibly the only reason to seek out the movie *Rhapsody in Blue*.
27 Goldberg and Garson, *George Gershwin: a Study in American Music*, 122.
28 Conducted by Marin Alsop. Angel CDC 0777 7 54851 2 7.
29 Mark Tucker discusses the different orchestrations in his unpublished paper "In Search of Will Vodery," which he was kind enough to let me read.
30 Goldberg and Garson, *George Gershwin: a Study in American Music*, 54.
31 Jablonski, *Gershwin*, 11.
32 *Gershwin: his Life and Music*, 55.
33 Mellers, *Music in a New Found Land*, 371.
34 Schuller, *Early Jazz*, 192. Schuller curiously credits Chester Hazlett rather than Russ Gorman with the clarinet glissando in the *Rhapsody*.
35 *Musings*, 44.
36 Darius Milhaud, *Notes Without Music*, 118–19, 35–37.
37 Osgood, *So this is Jazz*, 150.
38 *Ibid.*, 169.
39 Collier, *The Reception of Jazz in America*, 16.
40 PAST CD 9718.
41 Known to fans of *Some Like it Hot* as "Let's take a Stairway to the Stars."

5 Inception: the Aeolian Hall concert

1 Olin Downes, *New York Times*, 13 February 1924.

2 Goldberg and Garson, *George Gershwin: a Study in American Music*, 136.

3 W. H. Henderson, *New York Herald Tribune*, 5 March 1923.

4 Quoted in Ewen, *A Journey to Greatness*, 96–97. The complete program is reproduced in Schwartz, *Gershwin: his Life and Music*, 79.

5 Ewen, *A Journey to Greatness*, 97.

6 Goldberg and Garson, *George Gershwin: a Study in American Music*, 137.

7 Lopez's concert took place at the Metropolitan Opera House on 23 November 1924 and featured an original composition by W. C. Handy, "The Evolution of the Blues." But outside the concert hall Lopez beat Whiteman by two days with a lecture at the Anderson Art Galleries by Edward Burlingame Hill, professor of music at Harvard, on the history of jazz, illustrated by the Lopez band. The event was sponsored by the League of Composers.

8 Hagert, p.2 liner notes to *An Experiment in Modern Music*, 2.

9 It was probably a wishful misprint of Stransky. Edward Jablonski relates several Gershwin–Stravinsky tales in his book (*Gershwin*), though they sound third-hand.

10 Unnoted by the press was the fifteen-year-old Elliott Carter.

11 Ewen, *A Journey to Greatness*, 109.

12 (1) *An Experiment in Modern Music: Paul Whiteman at Aeolian Hall.* The Smithsonian Collection R028. Executive Producer Bill Bennett; programming and extensive annotation by Thornton Hagert, including a very interesting analysis of the *Rhapsody* as an "on-going process of music making". This is a reconstruction through recordings of the Whiteman Orchestra, the Original Dixieland Jazz Band, The Great White Way Orchestra, Art Hickman and his Orchestra, Zez Confrey, the Jean Goldkette Orchestra.

(2)*The Birth of Rhapsody in Blue: Paul Whiteman's Historic Aeolian Hall Concert of 1924*; Reconstructed and conducted by Maurice Peress with piano solos by Ivan Davis and Dick Hyman. Musical Heritage Society MHS 11238A; annotations by Peress. This is a "live" reconstruction based on parts from the Whiteman archives.

13 The Smithsonian reconstruction gives one chorus from an Art Hickman recording that contains much of the unkempt spontaneity that Whiteman had relegated to the past.

14 J. R. Taylor, liner notes to *Fletcher Henderson: Developing an American Orchestra 1923–1937*, Smithsonian Collection R006.

15 Liner notes to *The Birth of Rhapsody in Blue*, Musical Heritage Society 11238A.
16 Bergreen, *As Thousands Cheer: the Life of Irving Berlin*, 117.
17 Hagert, liner notes to *An Experiment in Modern Music*, 10.
18 Ewen, *A Journey to Greatness*, 115.

6 *Interpretations*

1 A contrast well documented in the four-CD set, *I Got Rhythm: the Music of George Gershwin* produced by the Smithsonian Collection of Recordings (RD 107/DMC4–1247).
2 Both of these are now available on CD: Pearl GEMM CDS 9483.
3 *The Gershwins*, 290.
4 Released on Nonesuch 9–79287–2.
5 CBS MK 42514.
6 RCA 6519–2-RG.
7 Sony SMK 47529.
8 *The Joy of Music*, 47–57.
9 CBS MK 42240.
10 CBS MK 39699.
11 Musical Heritage Society 11238A.
12 Bluebird 9785–2-RB.
13 On *Recollections of the Big Band Era*, Atlantic Jazz 7 90043–2.
14 Sony Classics SK68488. With the Orchestra of St. Luke's and the Lincoln Center Jazz Orchestra conducted by Robert Sadin.

7 *Influence*

1 *The New Republic*, 4 January 1933.
2 Thanks in particular to fine recordings by Nemi Jarvi and the Detroit Symphony Orchestra.
3 Walter Damrosch quoted in Goldberg and Garson, *George Gershwin: a Study in American Music*, 206.
4 See Wayne Shirley's "The Trial Orchestration of Gershwin's Concerto in F" and "Scoring the Concerto in F."
5 See Robert Wyatt, "The Seven Jazz Preludes of George Gershwin: a Historic Narrative," *American Music*, 7 (1989), 68–85.
6 Stearns and Stearns, *Jazz Dance*, 112.
7 With new lyrics by De Sylva, Brown and Henderson, the song became a hit in 1926 – after the *Concerto in F*.

8 *Aficionados* should seek out the Beiderbecke recording of the trumpet solo.
9 Orenstein, ed., *A Ravel Reader*, 294.
10 *Ibid.*, 293–94.
11 Ravel completed the Concerto in 1931; he had written two jazz pieces before meeting Gershwin: the fox-trot from *L'enfant et les sortilèges* (1920–25) and the Blues of the Violin Sonata (1923–27).
12 *A Virgil Thomson Reader*, 27.
13 Charters and Kunstadt, *Jazz: a History of the New York Scene*, 276.
14 The orchestration remains unpublished.
15 He recorded the song in October 1928 with the Gulf Coast Seven – which included Ellington regulars Tricky Sam Nanton, Johnny Hodges and Barney Bigard, and a racy vocal by lyricist Perry Bradford.
16 Willa Rouder, liner notes to *The Symphonic Jazz of James P. Johnson*, Musicmasters MMD 60066A.
17 Lewis, *When Harlem was in Vogue*, 173.
18 *Black Music in the Harlem Renaissance*, 14.
19 Tucker, *The Duke Ellington Reader*, 116–18.
20 Mark Tucker has called my attention to Ellington's 1926 composition "Rhapsody, Jr.," recorded by the Lunceford band in 1935, which "with its ninth and augmented chords, its whole-tone melodies and parallel triads . . . shows Ellington displaying some of the hallmarks of mid-twenties jazz modernism" *Ellington: the Early Years*, 199.
21 Collier, *Duke Ellington*, 145–48.
22 Quoted inTucker, *The Duke Ellington Reader*, 349.
23 Schuller, *Early Jazz*, 354.
24 Ewen, *A Journey to Greatness*, 211.
25 Quoted *ibid.*, 215.
26 See Gilbert, *The Music of Gershwin*, 152.
27 Gilbert discusses the Schillinger influence in detail, *ibid.*, 173–78.

8 Invisibility: ideology and reception

1 *So this is Jazz*, 186.
2 *American Mercury*, 4 (1925), 466.
3 "Gershwin and American Modernists," 646–68.
4 *An Hour with American Music*, 138.
5 *Copland*, 130. This view is contradicted on page 201 where Copland reports meeting Oscar Levant at a party at the Gershwins (*sic*) in 1932.
6 Copland, *Copland on Music*, 141.

7 See in particular the influential jazz criticism of Andre Hodeir, which echoes in the writings of Gunther Schuller and even LeRoi Jones.
8 As Richard Crawford has documented in *The American Musical Landscape*.
9 The absence of Whiteman and Grofé from recent jazz history opens a whole other can of worms; see James Lincoln Collier's *Reception of Jazz in America*.
10 *The Music of Black Americans*, 460.
11 *Music in a New Found Land*, 413.
12 Because his publisher had no idea if the music would sell, Gershwin received 80 per cent of the performance fees.
13 *The American Musical Landscape*, 65–66.
14 Bernstein and Levant continued to make the cuts from these recordings well into the 33 rpm era.
15 *New York Herald Tribune*, 13 February 1924.
16 *New York Herald Tribune*, 19 April 1946.
17 H. L. Mencken, *Baltimore Evening Sun*, 3 September 1934.
18 Thomson, *Virgil Thomson Reader*, 15–16.
19 F. Scott Fitzgerald, "Echoes of the Jazz Age," in *The Crack-Up*, 10–12.
20 *Terrible Honesty: Mongrel Manhattan in the 1920s*, 4.
21 *Ibid.*, 105.
22 *Yankee Blues*, 49.
23 *Ibid.*, 60.
24 Mason quoted in Moore, *ibid.*, 145.
25 *The Seven Lively Arts*, 264.
26 *Ibid.*, 92.
27 Armitage, ed., *George Gershwin*, 132.
28 *Vanity Fair*, April 1917.
29 Jablonski, *Gershwin Remembered*, 32.
30 Whiteman, *Jazz* (New York, 1926), 130–31.
31 *The Nation*, 5 March 1924.
32 *Modern Music*, 13/1 (November 1935), 18.
33 *Music Ho!* (London 1934/*R* 1985), 177–88.
34 *Yankee Blues*, p.71.
35 "Modernity: an Incomplete Project," 12.
36 *Terrible Honesty*, 70–71.
37 Adorno, *Quasi una Fantasia*, 50.
38 Adorno, *Sociology of Music*, 24.
39 *Art and Culture*, 10.
40 Dwight MacDonald, *Masscult and Midcult* (New York, 1961), 628.
41 Greenberg, "American Writing," in Rosenberg, *Mass Culture*, 879.

42 *No Respect*, 52.
43 *Gershwin: his Life and Music*, 24.
44 *World of Our Fathers*, 484.
45 *Ibid.*, 466.
46 *Ibid.*, 464.
47 *Ibid.*, 465.
48 *Ibid.*, 494.
49 Lifson, *The Yiddish Theater in America*, 343.
50 *World of our Fathers*, 488.
51 *Blues, Ideology, and Afro-American Literature*, 21.
52 Howe, *World of Our Fathers*, 563.
53 *Ibid.*
54 "Blackface, White Noise," 439.
55 Howe, *World of Our Fathers*, 563.
56 Sanders, "The American Popular Song," in Villiers, ed., *Next Year in Jerusalem*, 202.
57 "Blackface, White Noise," 439.
58 Alpert, *The Life and Times of Porgy and Bess*, 75.
59 See Gabler, *An Empire of their Own*, 300–01.
60 *Virgil Thomson Reader*, 411.
61 *Culture as History*, 206.

Select Bibliography

Adorno, Theodor W. "The Culture Industry Reconsidered," in *Critical Theatre and Society*, ed. Stephen Eric Bronner and Douglas MacKay Kellner (New York and London, 1989)

Introduction to the Sociology of Music, trans. E. B. Ashton (New York, 1962)

Philosophy of Modern Music, trans. Anne G. Mitchell and Wesley V. Blomster (New York, 1985)

Prisms, trans. Samuel Weber and Sherry Weber (Cambridge, Mass., 1967)

Quasi Una Fantasia: Essays on Modern Music, trans. Rodney Livingstone (London and New York, 1963)

Alpert, Hollis. *The Life and Times of Porgy and Bess: the Story of an American Classic* (New York, 1990)

Armitage, Merle, ed. *George Gershwin* (New York, 1938)

Badger, Reid. *A Life in Ragtime: a Biography of James Reese Europe* (New York and Oxford, 1995)

Baker, Houston A., Jr. *Modernism and the Harlem Renaissance* (Chicago and London, 1987)

Blues, Ideology, and Afro-American Literature: a Vernacular Theory (Chicago and London, 1984)

Bergreen, Laurence. *As Thousands Cheer: the Life of Irving Berlin* (New York, 1991)

Berlin, Edward A. *Ragtime: a Musical and Cultural History* (Berkeley, Los Angeles and London, 1980)

Bernstein, Leonard. *The Joy of Music* (New York, 1954)

Blesh, Rudi. *Shining Trumpets: a History of Jazz* (New York, 1946)

Bordman, Gerald. *American Musical Theatre: a Chronicle* (New York and Oxford, 1978)

Jerome Kern: his Life and Music (New York and Oxford, 1980)

Brown, R. L. "William Grant Still, Florence Price, and William Dawson: Echoes of the Harlem Renaissance," in *Black Music in the Harlem Renaissance*, ed. Samuel A. Floyd Jr. (Knoxville, Tenn., 1993)

Bushell, Garvin and Mark Tucker. *Jazz From the Beginning* (Ann Arbor, Mich., 1988)

Charters, Samuel B. and Leonard Kunstadt. *Jazz: a History of the New York Scene* (New York, 1962)

Collier, James Lincoln. *Duke Ellington* (New York and Oxford, 1987)

The Reception of Jazz in America: a New View (New York, 1988)

Copland, Aaron. *Copland On Music,* (London, 1944)

The New Music: 1900–1960 (New York, 1968)

Copland, Aaron and Vivian Perlis. *Copland: 1900 through 1942* (New York, 1984)

Crawford, Richard. *The American Musical Landscape* (Berkeley, Los Angeles and London, 1993)

Davis, Francis. *The History of the Blues: the Roots, the Music, the People from Charley Payton to Robert Cray* (New York, 1995)

DeLong, Thomas A. *Pops: Paul Whiteman, King of Jazz* (Piscataway, NJ, 1983)

Douglas, Ann. *Terrible Honesty: Mongrel Manhattan in the 1920s* (New York, 1995)

Ennis, Philip H. *The Seventh Stream: the Emergence of Rocknroll in American Popular Music* (Hanover and London, 1992)

Ewen, David. *A Journey to Greatness: the Life and Music of George Gershwin* (New York, 1956)

Firestone, Ross. *Swing, Swing, Swing: the Life and Times of Benny Goodman* (New York and London, 1993)

Fitzgerald, F. Scott. *The Crack-Up* (Middlesex, 1965)

Floyd, Samuel A., ed. *Black Music in the Harlem Renaissance* (Tennessee, 1993)

Furia, Phillip. *The Poets of Tin Pan Alley: a History of America's Great Lyricists* (New York and Oxford, 1990)

Gabler, Neal. *An Empire of their Own: How the Jews Invented Hollywood* (New York, 1988)

George, Nelson. *The Death of Rhythm and Blues* (New York, 1988)

Gilbert, Steven E. *The Music of Gershwin* (New Haven and London, 1995)

Goldberg, Isaac and Edith Garson. *George Gershwin: a Study in American Music* (New York, 1958)

Goldberg, Isaac. *Tin Pan Alley* (New York, 1961)

Goldman, Richard Franko. *Selected Essays and Reviews 1948–1968*, ed. Dorothy Klotzman (New York, 1967)

Graziano, J. "Black Musical Theatre and the Harlem Renaissance Movement," in *Black Music in the Harlem Renaissance*, ed. Samuel A. Floyd Jr. (Knoxville, Tenn., 1993)

Greenberg, Clement. *Art and Culture* (Boston, 1961)

Habermas, J. "Modernity: an Incomplete Project," in *The Anti-Aesthetic: Essays on Postmodern Culture*, ed. Hal Foster (Port Townsend, Wash., 1983)

Hagert, Thornton, liner notes for *An Experiment in Modern Music: Paul Whiteman at Aeolian Hall*, The Smithsonian Collection R028

Hamm, Charles. *Yesterdays: Popular Song in America* (New York and London, 1983)

Handy, W. C. *Blues: an Anthology* (New York, 1990)

Hart, Philip. *Orpheus in the New World* (New York, 1973)

Hitchcock, H. Wiley. *Music in the United States: a Historical Introduction* (Englewood Cliffs, NJ., 1969)

Howe, Irving. *World of Our Fathers: the Journey of the East European Jews to America and the Life they Found and Made* (New York, 1976)

Huggins, Nathan Irvin. *Harlem Renaissance* (London, Oxford and New York, 1971)

Hyland, William G. *The Song is Ended: Songwriters and American Music 1900–1950* (New York and Oxford, 1995)

Jablonski, Edward. *Gershwin: a Biography* (New York, 1987)

Gershwin Remembered (Portland, Oreg., 1992)

Jones, LeRoi. *Blues People: Negro Music in White America* (New York, 1963)

Kimball, Robert, and Simon, Albert. *The Gershwins* (New York, 1973)

Lederman, Minna. *The Life and Death of a Small Magazine* (New York, 1983)

Leonard, Neil. *Jazz and the White Americans* (Chicago and London, 1962)

Lester, James. *Too Marvelous for Words: the Life and Genius of Art Tatum* (New York and Oxford, 1994)

Levant, Oscar. *The Memoirs of an Amnesiac* (Hollywood, Calif., 1989)

Levine, Lawrence W. *Highbrow Lowbrow: the Emergence of Cultural Hierarchy in America* (Cambridge, Mass., and London, 1988)

Lewis, David Levering. *When Harlem was in Vogue* (New York and Oxford, 1979)

Lifson, David S. *The Yiddish Theatre in America* (New York and London, 1965)

Machlin, Paul S. *Stride: the Music of Fats Waller* (Boston, 1985)

Mellers, Wilfrid. *Music in a New Found Land* (New York, 1964)

Milhaud, Darius. *Notes Without Music* (New York, 1953)

Moore, Macdonald Smith. *Yankee Blues: Musical Culture and American Identity* (Bloomington, Ind., 1985)

Murray, Albert. *Stomping the Blues* (New York, 1976)

Ogren, Kathy J. *The Jazz Revolution: Twenties America and the Meaning of Jazz* (New York and Oxford, 1989)

Oja, Carol. "Gershwin and American Modernists of the 1920s," *The Musical Quarterly*, 78 (1994), 646–68

Orenstein, Arbie., ed. *A Ravel Reader: Correspondence, Articles, Interviews* (New York, 1990)

Orenstein, Arbie. *Ravel: Man and Musician* (New York, 1968)

Osgood, Henry O. *So this is Jazz* (Boston, 1926)

Peyser, Joan. *The Memory of All That: the Life of George Gershwin* (New York and London, 1993)

Pleasants, Henry. *The Agony of Modern Music* (New York, 1955)

Porter, Lewis, Michael Ullman, and Edward Hazell. *Jazz: From its Origins to the Present* (Englewood Cliffs, NJ, 1993)

Riddle, R. "Novelty Piano Music," in *Ragtime: its History, Composers, and Music*, ed. John Edward Hasse (New York, 1985)

Riis, Thomas L. *Just Before Jazz: Black Musical Theatre in New York, 1890 to 1915* (Washington and London, 1989)

Rodgers, Richard. *Musical Stages: An Autobiography* (New York, 1975)

Rogin, M. "Blackface, White Noise: the Jewish Jazz Singer Finds His Voice," *Critical Inquiry*, 18 (1992), 417–53

Rorem, Ned. *Settling the Score: Essays on Music* (New York and London, 1988)

Rosenberg, Bernard and David Manning White. *Mass Culture: Popular Arts in America* (Glencoe, Ill., 1957)

Rosenberg, Deena. *Fascinating Rhythm: the Collaboration of George and Ira Gershwin* (London, 1992)

Rosenfield, Paul. *An Hour with American Music* (Philadelphia and London, 1929)

Ross, Andrew. *No Respect: Intellectuals and Popular Culture* (New York and London, 1989)

Salzman, Eric. *Twentieth-Century Music: an Introduction* (Englewood Cliffs, NJ, 1967)

Sanjek, Russell and David. *American Popular Music Business in the 20th Century* (New York and Oxford, 1991)

Schuller, Gunther. *Early Jazz: its Roots and Musical Development* (New York and Oxford, 1968)

Musings: the Musical Worlds of Gunther Schuller (New York and Oxford, 1986)

The Swing Era: the Development of Jazz 1930–1945 (New York and Oxford, 1989)

Schwartz, Charles. *Gershwin: his Life and Music* (New York, 1973)

Seldes, Gilbert. *The Seven Lively Arts* (New Aork, 1962)

Shipton, A. *Fats Waller* (New York, 1988)

Shirley, Wayne. "Scoring the Concerto in F" *American Music*, 3/3 (1985), 277–98

"The Trial Orchestration of Gershwin's Concerto in F," *Notes*, 39/3 (1983), 570

Southern, Eileen. *Readings in Black American Music* (New York and London, 1983)
The Music of Black Americans: a History (New York, 1971)
Stearns, Marshall and Jean. *Jazz Dance: the Story of American Vernacular Dance* (New York and London, 1968)
Susman, Warren I. *Culture as History: the Transformation of American Society in the Twentieth Century* (New York, 1984)
Thomson, Virgil. *A Virgil Thomson Reader* (New York, 1981)
Music Reviewed 1940–1954 (New York, 1967)
The Art of Judging Music (New York, 1948)
Tucker, Mark. *Ellington: the Early Years* (Urbana and Chicago, 1991)
"In Search of Will Vodery," unpublished paper (1996)
The Duke Ellington Reader (New York and Oxford, 1993)
Vance, Joel. *Fats Waller: his Life and Times* (London, 1979)
Varèse, Louise. *Varèse: a Looking-Glass Diary, Volume I: 1883–1928* (New York, 1972)
Villiers, Douglas. *Next Year In Jerusalem* (New York and London, 1976)
Whitcomb, Ian. *Irving Berlin and Ragtime America* (New York, 1987)
Wilder, Alec. *American Popular Song: the Great Innovators 1900–1950*, ed. James T. Maher (New York, 1972)
Wilk, Max. *They're Playing Our Song: the Truth Behind the Words and Music of Three Generations* (Mount Kisco, New York and London, 1991)
Woll, Allen. *Black Musical Theatre: from Coontown to Dreamgirls* (Baton Rouge, La., 1989)

Index

Note: As befits the index to a book about a piece which defies classification, a hybrid approach has been adopted. Songs will be found under their titles; those by Gershwin also appear in his entry. "Classical" works appear under their composers; the *Rhapsody in Blue* has its own entry. Subheadings for works follow other subheadings where applicable.

Credits

RHAPSODY IN BLUE™

By GEORGE GERSHWIN

Musical extracts appear as follows.

Rhapsody in Blue by George Gershwin. © 1924, 1939 WB Music Corp. (Renewed). All Rights Reserved. Used by Permission. Warner Bros. Publications, Inc., Miami, Fla. 33014

"I Was so Young (You Were So Beautiful)" by George Gershwin, Irving Caesar and Alfred Bryan. © WB Music Corp. (Renewed). All Rights Reserved. Used by Permission. Warner Bros. Publications, Inc., Miami, Fla. 33014

"Swanee" by George Gershwin, Irving Caesar. © 1919 WB Music Corporation and Irving Caesar Music (Renewed). All Rights Administered by WB Music Corp. All Rights Reserved. Used by Permission. Warner Bros. Publications, Inc., Miami, Fla. 33014

"I Got Rhythm" by Ira Gershwin, George Gershwin. © 1930 WB Music Corp. (Renewed). All Rights Reserved. Used by Permission. Warner Bros. Publications, Inc., Miami, Fla. 33014

Second Rhapsody by George Gershwin. © 1932 WB Music Corp. (Renewed). All Rights Reserved. Used by Permission. Warner Bros. Publications, Inc., Miami, Fla. 33014

Concerto in F by George Gershwin. © 1927 WB Music Corp. (Renewed). All Rights Reserved. Used by Permission. Warner Bros. Publications, Inc., Miami, Fla. 33014